HOW TO
RECRUIT
GREAT
BOARD
MEMBERS

A GUIDE FOR NONPROFIT AGENCIES

Text by Dorian Dodson
Illustrations and Design by Janice St. Marie

Published by
Adolfo Street Publications
Post Office Box 490
Santa Fe, New Mexico 87504-0490
(505) 473-4433

ISBN # 0-9632445-1-5
Library of Congress Catalog Card Number: 93-071372

Publisher's Cataloging in Publication
(Prepared by Quality Books Inc.)

Dodson, Dorian.
    How to recruit great board members: a guide for
nonprofit agencies / Dorian Dodson.
    p. cm.
    ISBN 0-9632445-1-5

    1. Nonprofit organizations--Management. 2. Directors of
corporations. I. Title.

HD62.6.D63H6 1993   658'.048
                                 QBI93-645

This book is dedicated to everyone
who has ever looked, high and low,
for great board members.

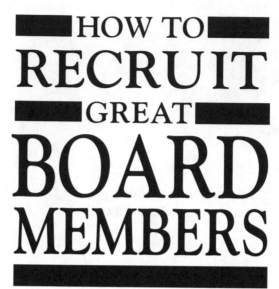

HOW TO RECRUIT GREAT BOARD MEMBERS

A GUIDE FOR NONPROFIT AGENCIES

INTRODUCTION

You must have good board members

1

What are the three most important elements of a strong nonprofit agency? Of course, you need good staff and you need money. Without these two critical ingredients, your agency will go nowhere. But what else do you need?

You must have good board members. They are just as important as qualified staff and sufficient funds. And, like these other two precious commodities, good board members are very hard to come by. But you already know that.

The purpose of this guide is to give you some basic, practical advice on how to find good board members and get them to serve on your board. The guide will give you ideas on how to hold on to them once you have them. It will also provide you with some ideas on how you can best use the time and talents of people who may wish to help you but who are not ready to join the board—at least not yet.

The last section contains sample recruitment letters, brochures, press releases and public service announcements geared toward recruitment of board members. Feel free to use them as they are or to modify them to fit your agency's unique situation.

Why did we write this guide and what will it offer you? In one way or another, we (your author and all of the people whose experiences make up the "we" in this book) have worked with nonprofit agencies for over sixteen years. When funding and overseeing these organizations, we were struck by how badly agencies needed good board members and how difficult it was to find them. As chief executive staff of different nonprofit agencies, we remember how much easier (and more pleasant) it was to function with a good solid board. On the other hand, we would

rather forget the days when we were more likely to
see Halley's comet than a quorum at a board meeting.

Finally, as board members ourselves, we know how important it is to have a first-rate team to guide an agency. Being on a dynamic, hard working board is a great experience. Being stuck on a weak, inactive and whiny board made your author wonder if, in a previous life, she had pulled the wings off helpless insects to deserve such punishment.

A good nonprofit makes a very important contribution to its clients and community. And, like everything else, nonprofits need strong and solid foundations. Your nonprofit will only be as strong as the board that is running it. Note: Throughout this guide we have used examples from personal experiences and observations. All of them are dramatic but all of them are true (although the names of the people and agencies have been changed). We include them to underscore different points and to show you that there is a lot of the good, bad, ugly and amusing going on out there in the world of board recruitment.

SOME BASIC DEFINITIONS
Before we begin our discussion on recruitment of board members, let's agree upon some common definitions to be sure we are all talking about the same thing. Please bear with us if we repeat some information you already know.

Nonprofit: An agency approved as a nonprofit corporation through the commission or attorney general's office in the state in which it conducts business. There will be articles of incorporation, by-laws, probably a tax-exempt status from the Internal Revenue Service and so on. We will use the terms agency, organization and nonprofit interchangeably.

Nonprofits can make money. However, revenues earned by nonprofits are not returned to stockholders, shareholders, partners or owners. Instead, they are used by the agency in some way to further its mission.

Board of Directors: The governing body of the nonprofit. As such, the board has the ultimate authority and responsibility for the organization. We will call this the board of directors or simply the board. We will not talk about advisory councils or other committees that may have input (but not authority) into the organization's operations. However, you may find much of this discussion helpful in recruiting advisory committee members as well.

Funding Source: The entity (federal, state, local or private) providing funds to a nonprofit.

Mission: The overall purpose or underlying reason for the agency's existence.

You: This is probably the first time you have seen *you* defined! In this guide, the word "you" means board members, executive staff members or any other persons who wish to increase the number and/ or quality of their agency's board members. So, we will assume you have a strong commitment to the agency and its mission.

With these definitions in mind, it is time to look at the steps we need to recruit board members successfully.

WHO ARE YOU, WHERE ARE YOU AND WHAT DO YOU DO?

Know your agency before you begin
to recruit board members

2

These are important questions and you have probably already given the answers a lot of thought. But it is time to ask and answer them again in the context of board recruitment. Knowing your organization is one of the first (and most important) steps in attracting and keeping good board members.

WHO ARE YOU?

First, you need a mission statement. More to the point, you need a mission. If your articles of incorporation and by-laws do not have a strong mission statement, you should develop one. Why? Because you cannot expect others to understand what you are doing (why your agency exists) if *you* cannot articulate its basic purpose.

We have seen good potential board members lose interest quickly because they could not get a straight answer to their questions about the agency's mission and purpose. The following is a verbatim conversation from a board recruitment session we attended several years ago.

Jim Smith (board president):
"Well, Bob, I am very happy to have the opportunity to meet with you. I am glad you have decided to join our agency's board."

Robert Jones (potential board member):
"Thank you. But I haven't completely made up my mind as to which board I will join. I moved here late last year and I have been wanting to get more involved in community activities. I think being on the board of a good nonprofit agency would be a great way to start. I am a certified public accountant, you know, and I have a lot of experience in working with nonprofits in different parts of the country."

(At this point, Jim Smith should have been doing triple back flips. Having an experienced accountant on a nonprofit board of directors is every agency's dream come true.)

Jim:
"Oh, that's nice. We have never had an accountant on the board. Well, let me tell you all about us. We meet once a month and we have our annual meeting in July. Sometimes we go to a really great beach hotel for a couple of days and—"

Robert:
"Jim, what I am really interested in is the agency's purpose. What are you all about, so to speak?"

(By the way, accountants are generally tightfisted with money. They are supposed to be. The last thing you would do with an accountant is talk about going to a fancy resort for board meetings. That, unfortunately, was the first thing Jim did.)

Jim:

"Well, let's see. We take seniors to doctor appointments, help them find housing, at least I think we still do that, visit anyone who is homebound, that sort of thing."

Robert:

"But what is the agency's primary goal? To provide supportive services for seniors? To advocate for them?"

Jim:

"Well, I guess you could say that. Sometimes we hold a dinner for them and get a good caterer in. Makes them feel important, you know."

Robert (a little taken aback):

"I can see that a lot of money is spent on social events, but I am still not sure I understand what the agency's goal is. Do you have a charter or mission statement I could read?"

Jim (still not getting the hint):

"Oh, there's one in the articles of incorporation, I think, but to be honest with you, Bob, it has been so long since I read it. But last year we took some of them on a moonlight cruise around the island. Wife and kids went along, too!"

Robert (not a happy man):

"Well, Jim, I really need to be going. I am going to talk to a couple of other agencies and I will get back to you."

Robert leaves.

****

That *really* happened. One of us pretended to drop something under the table so she could laugh hysterically. The other just stared bug-eyed and slack-jawed at Jim in amazement, especially when he said "I wonder what made him leave so quickly . . . and I hadn't really begun to tell him all of the great things we do!"

However, it is not always that bad. Some people do an excellent job of talking to prospective candidates. Let's contrast this with another scene we witnessed less than six months later . . .

Candy Altura (executive director):
"Well, Ms. St. James, thanks for making time for me in your busy schedule. By the way, I know you work for the XYZ Foundation, and I know what the Foundation does. But what exactly do you do there?"

Janice St. James:
"Please call me Janice. I am a fund raiser for the Foundation. But I am interested in working with a nonprofit agency in this town. I think it is time I direct some of my energies toward the community I live in."

(Candy knows Janice is a potential gold mine. A skilled fund raiser is a tremendous asset to any organization.)

Candy:
"Well, we could certainly use you on our board! Fund-raising is, to be frank, one of our weakest links. But it is also something that the board recently listed as one of its major goals for the upcoming year. What information can I give you about our agency?"

Janice:
   "I am very interested in your overall goal or mission. What is it you hope to accomplish?"

Candy:
   "Let me give you a little history. In 1982, a group of very dedicated advocates realized that older poor people in this area were having a rough time of it. They had little or no access to decent medical care, affordable housing or even nutritious meals. And, of course, their right to lead a dignified life was totally compromised. So, they formed Uptown, Inc. to help very poor senior citizens in this town and surrounding areas live decent, safe and healthy lives. We do this through direct services, assistance, advocacy and lobbying at the state and federal level. I have the mission statement here in our new pamphlet for you to review at your leisure. However, that is us in a nutshell."

Janice:
"I'm impressed. That is a very worthy goal and I can see how you could use all of the funds you can get. I think I could help you and I certainly would be proud to work with an agency with such an important mission. This is just the kind of project I could really sink my teeth into!"

****

Janice did join the board and, within two years, raised a lot of money for the organization. Obviously, Candy did an excellent job stating the agency's mission. But Candy was reflecting what was already a well articulated and clear goal.

In our experience, such examples are common. Agencies without an articulated mission have a hard time attracting good board members. There are a lot of Jim Smiths out there who list activities and events when they should be talking missions and goals.

On the other hand, if an agency board and staff know what they are all about, they are much better able to recruit high-powered individuals to sit on their boards. Their purpose, professionalism and dedication are immediately obvious and very compelling.

So, if you have not done so already, define your mission. (Remember: A mission can change over time. The important thing is to be on top of the change.) Then make sure everyone involved with the agency who might come in contact with potential board members knows exactly what that mission is. It helps to have it written down in a brochure or an agency fact sheet. If you need to, dust off and update your articles of incorporation and by-laws. Make sure these key documents reflect the agency's current mission.

WHERE ARE YOU?

This question has two different and equally important meanings. The first and most obvious is where your agency is *physically* located. Are you in a large metropolitan city or in a small, rural community? You will, of course, have more choices of potential board members in larger cities. There are simply more people to choose from. However, it is harder to be recognized in a large city because there are usually many well established agencies doing work that is at least somewhat similar. You have to stand out if you want to attract good board members.

What makes your agency different from the others? Why should someone join your board as opposed to the one down the street? In addition to a solid mission statement, the staff and board of agencies in large cities must recognize and articulate what makes their organization different from others with a similar purpose. Like any other "product" on the market competing for attention, people in urban agencies must know and express what makes their agencies better than all of the rest.

If you are in a small, rural town, you will have the opposite problem. The chances are there are not a lot of other agencies in the area doing anything even remotely similar. However, you have far fewer people to draw upon as potential board members.

In the smaller towns, you are also more likely to see people sit on a number of boards at once. (Although this phenomenon also occurs in larger towns, it is much more common in the smaller communities.) If one agency finds a good board member, other agencies will probably try to recruit him or her as well.

We have mixed feelings on this point. There are semi-professional board members who spend a lot of time attending board meetings. The positive side is they become quite skilled at the business of running boards. The down side is they sometimes lose their enthusiasm for the goals of the agencies they represent. They are caught up in the glamour of being a board member and they forget that the agency is there to fulfil a mission. Some of them even become board "groupies." They spend their lives sitting on boards.

If you are located in a smaller community, you probably don't have to worry about being different, but you *will* have to work at digging up top notch board members. Then you have to work at keeping them from being snatched up by every other organization within a 500 hundred-mile radius.

The large city and the small, rural town are the obvious extremes. Your agency may be in a community somewhere in the middle. Assessing your agency in light of its location will help you focus your recruitment strategies. Of course, regardless of where your agency is located, it never hurts to be able to show why you are different from all the rest and to know how to look for good potential board members instead of waiting for them to come to you.

****

The other half of **WHERE ARE YOU?** is the life cycle of your organization. In this context, life cycle means the stage of development of the agency at any given time. Agencies can be new or young, mature or very mature. The life cycle will also influence the type of board member you want (as well as the type of board member who will be interested in you).

The New or Young Organization
If your agency is very young, there is one kind of board member you *must* have. Founding board members must be enthusiastic, energetic and committed. At this point in the organization's existence, that is usually all there is—a bunch of board members determined to make it work. There is no staff, no budget and no program in place. Even after staff, funding and office space have been secured, there is a lot for the board members to do. And, of course, they must be sure the agency becomes thoroughly saturated in the mission as they envisioned it.

We know some wonderful, exciting people who started agencies and sat on the founding boards. They met until two or three in the morning for days or weeks on end. They went through endless sheets of newsprint taped to the walls hammering out mission statements, articles of incorporation, procedures and budgets. They gave up weekends and holidays to put their vision into practice. Without these dynamos, the organizations would never have gotten off the ground.

The Mature Organization
Of course, any agency will benefit from enthusiastic and dedicated board members. But mature agencies *must* have board members who are experienced in running businesses because that is what an established, funded and fully staffed agency is—a business. (By the way, we are of the school of thought that says a nonprofit should be run like a

good business. Even if the bottom line is not a dollar return to the stockholders or the owners, a nonprofit will benefit from sound business and organizational practices. Business should not be a dirty word. But we digress.)

There are some excellent books and periodicals about the for profit business world that talk about the life cycles, evolution and culture of companies. (Please see the bibliography at the end of the book.) We learned a lot from them that we apply to our dealings with nonprofits. They remind us that the people who have the genius and drive to start a successful company are often not the best ones to run it later on. We think the same principles hold true for nonprofits. Founding board members are often not the ones who can successfully guide an agency in its later stages.

The Very Mature Organization or the Agency in a Prolonged Crisis

Very mature agencies (organizations in their golden years?) often need revitalization which takes yet another type of board member. These are special people. They have the burning enthusiasm reminiscent of good founding board members but the seasoned maturity of experienced board members. They manage to light fires under people who have been complacent for years. At the same time, however, they are realistic and practical.

An agency with some major weaknesses or in an ongoing crisis needs solid, stable board members who are prepared to weather the storm and remain calm. To a certain extent, a nonprofit becomes a self-contained universe. If a crisis hits (sudden uncertainty in future funding, the resignation of a key staff person under suspicious circumstances, a lawsuit filed by clients), everyone in this small universe goes ballistic. As a result, whatever trouble the agency is in is compounded by the staff and board reaction. If (and we hope it never happens) you find yourself in this unfortunate situation, there are three things you should do. First, remain calm yourself. Second, strongly encourage everyone else to do the same. Third, if you have a board vacancy, look for someone immediately who can help stabilize the situation. Sometimes it is much easier for an outsider or new person to take on this absolutely vital role.

Consider your own agency's life cycle when you develop your recruitment efforts. As we said before, mature agencies need enthusiasm and young agencies will benefit from seasoned professionals. But, like all living things, there are different primary needs at different stages.

WHO IS ALREADY ON YOUR BOARD?

Take an inventory of your current board roster. If you already have a dynamite fund raiser but no one with solid fiscal or management experience, it would be foolish to spend a lot of time and effort recruiting a second fund-raising giant. To the extent that you can, you should try to balance the skills (and even personalities) of your board members.

WHAT DO YOU WANT TO DO?

You may think this is a question with an obvious answer. After all, you have already defined your mission statement, right? And you should assume that anyone who joins your board wants the same thing, right? True, but that is not the whole story. There are many different roads to reach your destination. Again we will use extremes to dramatize our point.

In every movement, cause or issue you will find the radicals and the conservatives. (We are *not* using these terms in the current political context in which radicals are at the far left and conservatives are at the extreme right of the spectrum. We are talking about people with almost opposite approaches to a common goal. They have the same destination. What they do to get there, however, can be as different as the climate at the North Pole and the Equator.)

In this context, radicals think the time to make things happen is TODAY, not five or ten years from now. They tell us we must act now because tomorrow will be too late. Conservatives think change cannot and will not happen overnight. They advocate a much more gradual evolution which they believe will bring more lasting change.

Think of the environmental movement. (For a moment, put aside your feelings, pro or con, about
environmentalists. Look at this as an example of
different approaches.) There are people and organizations blocking whaling ships or strapping themselves to ancient trees earmarked for the chain saw.
They say if we don't act now there will be no whales
or ancient trees to protect.

There are other people and organizations trying to
develop grassroots movements at the community
level to bring about a change in awareness and
perspective. They feel aggressive actions will alienate the very people they want to win over.

Who is right? We think there is room (in fact, a
compelling need) for both in almost every cause. To
continue our example: Without immediate action,
certain species *will* be lost forever before enough
people are committed to their preservation. However, without a long-term commitment to preserve
the ecological diversity of the planet, environmentalists will have to wage ecowarfare every time a
particular species of plant or animal is on the brink of
extinction.

Once again, there are few pure extremes. But you
get the point. Be sure of the path your organization
wants to take to fulfill its mission. Then be sure you
communicate that to prospective board members. In
our example, the person who wants something to
happen right now will not be content passing out
literature at town meetings for the next ten years.
Conversely, it would be a great shock to gentle, non
assertive souls to find themselves chained to a tree
with some very angry lumberjacks less than ten feet
away.

Your Agency

There are other ways in which people with presumably the same mission can disagree. Mission statements can mean dramatically different things to different people.

For example, let's say the overall mission of your agency is to help the homeless. You meet a potential board candidate who says he really believes in helping the homeless and he wants to sign up right away. Your agency wants to develop affordable permanent housing for homeless families in safe and decent neighborhoods. On the other hand, the candidate feels helping the homeless means opening up more shelters.

The difference here is more profound than may be obvious. Those who think the answer to the homeless problem is to build more affordable permanent housing often believe that building more shelters will only result in "warehousing" the homeless and avoiding the real problems. Those who want to build more shelters see this as a perfectly logical thing to do— people have no place to go and they need a roof over their head. Shelters, they think, are a logical solution.

The agency board and this candidate both think they know best how to help the homeless. However, there is a real difference between them. One looks at the long-term, permanent solution. The other looks at the immediate need.

Anybody with even half a brain will be impressed if you are clear about all of these things. You will be able to will give them the information they need to make a good decision about joining your board. It will also make you look much more professional. So, if they join, it will be for the right reasons. And if they

26

don't join, both you and they will be happier in the long run.

****

It is time for a little straight talk. We assume you *are* trying to recruit people who do have some brainpower. But we have seen several organizations create what can only be described as rubber-stamp boards. (A rubber-stamp board is one which never questions or challenges and does not exercise its authority. It does not set the course for the agency—instead, it follows the course set by others without question.) It may be that one or two board members (or perhaps the executive director) are trying to run the show. The agencies' goals were very commendable and, in the majority of these cases, the architects of these passive boards were probably just trying to make their job easier. It can be very tempting but it is not the way to go.

In the long run, these boards hurt their agencies and, therefore, their missions. Outsiders can tell immediately if there is a bunch of deadheads on the board and will lose respect for the organization. Funding sources will become suspicious and nervous about the stability of the organization. And, you will not be able to attract the kind of brainpower and commitment you truly need.

Finally, even rubber-stamp board members find some backbone at times when you least expect it. But because they have never been active before, they really don't know what to do and they often make a terrible mess of things. If a crisis hits, these formerly quiet and submissive board members go nuts. They start to micromanage the agency and they can make very poor decisions.

So, if you ever find yourself wishing for board members who will simply show up and nod their heads at whatever you say, don't give in to the temptation! Always go for the best you can get.

DEFINING THE MUTUAL EXPECTATIONS

Why do you want them and
why should they join your agency?

3

The previous section can be summed up in two words—know thyself. It is essential. Once you have gone through the process of self (agency) reckoning, you are ready to recruit the right people to sit on your board. In this section, we will focus on the bottom line—why do you want them? Just as important, what do you have to offer and what do you expect from them?

1. Why do you want them?

In the previous section, we advised you to take an inventory of your current board. Assuming you have done so, you should be able to answer this question. You must also be able to convey this information to prospective board members.

If you have recruited people because of their specific experience or skills, you should let them know that up front. One board we know recruited a locally popular country-and-western singer. The singer thought she was being asked to sit on the board because of her reputation. In reality, the agency board and staff had visions of her singing (for free, of course) at every benefit, dinner and dance they intended to hold for the next five years. *That* relationship did not last very long!

On the other hand, we know of agencies that identified specific needs and looked for potential board members who could meet those needs. Again, honest and up front communications (beginning with clear expectations) made all of the difference in the world. "Our agency needs a good accountant on the board to guide us in the anticipated period of rapid growth in our budget. You, Mr. or Ms. CPA, have an excellent reputation working with nonprofits. We would really like you to sit on our board." Everyone knows where he or she stands.

Depending upon your funding sources, you may be required to have specific representation on your board from the various ethnic groups in (or different sectors of) your community. Even if you are not, your board must represent the people or cause that it serves. An agency in business to assist refugees from other countries should have substantial representation from its client population (refugees) sitting on its board. An agency providing services to an inner-city neighborhood would be ill advised and would lack all credibility if it did not have people from the community it served sitting on its board. An agency formed to address specific women's issues would be the laughing stock of the community if it had no women (in fact, if it did not have a majority of women) on its governing board.

All of these factors influence why an agency wants or needs certain board members and there is nothing wrong with this type of careful and objective analysis and recruitment process. However, you must never treat anyone you recruit to sit on your board as a token or the person you point to when you need to demonstrate your compliance, open-mindedness, competency or ethics.

Unfortunately, we have seen this happen much too often. An agency in major fiscal trouble showcased the certified public accountant who was talked into joining the board two weeks before. An organization situated in a neighborhood in which the population was over 90% African-American pointed to its one African-American board member as proof of its concern for the neighborhood it served.

No one is fooled by this kind of charade. Funding sources see right through it and the people you have recruited figure it out very fast when they have been asked to sit on the board because of what they represent, not who they are or what they have to contribute.

You must be sincere and honest in your recruitment efforts. We hope you genuinely want people on your board of different ethnic backgrounds and skills and people who represent the community you serve. They will make the best contributions of all if you have recruited them for the right reasons.

As board members, your clients have a unique perspective. They know what it is like to receive services from your agency. They know how the staff treats them when there are no mucky-mucks around. They know if the concern and respect for clients is genuine or just so much lip service for the sake of funding sources and the media. They know if the organization is really doing the job it set out to do.

31

Agency clients are frequently the toughest and best board members of all. Why? Because they, more than anyone else, see the organization's mission clearly ahead of them and can be very impatient with the numerous obstacles that always seem to get in the way of reaching the mission. Use that impatience to the agency's advantage—it provides honesty and momentum and helps you get down to the important stuff.

2. What do you have to offer?

When you recruit board members, you will obviously want to appeal to their altruistic nature. Your agency is doing something positive to make this a better world. Whether you are helping senior citizens, troubled teenagers or an endangered species, or trying to stop drunk driving, your organization is making an important contribution. And that should be a primary selling point. Your mission statement, clearly articulated and, we hope, packaged in a nice (it doesn't have to be expensive) pamphlet should "sell" potential board members on the contribution you are making. Reinforce the fact that they will be part of this important mission if they join your board.

However, 99 percent of all people need something more than just knowing they are helping a worthy cause. These are not selfish, materialistic jerks, but they are human beings. It is only normal and natural for them to need and want some other type of reward for spending their time, energy and possibly their money on your organization.

The trick is for you to recognize that fact, figure out what else you have to sell and include it in your sales pitch. As part of your pamphlet, you might even list the key benefits and rewards of being on your board.

Here is just a partial list of things you may have to offer that would be attractive to good board prospects.

A. It is a great opportunity to develop job-related and interpersonal skills. Good board members need to know a lot about budgets, supervision, public speaking and many other topics. They must also be diplomats and fund raisers, politicians and advocates. If they are unskilled in these areas, they will get a crash course that money could not buy. More experienced people will find a never ending opportunity to refine their skills and gain additional knowledge. All of this looks good on a job resume, an application for graduate school and even on a list of credentials for public office.

B. It is a great opportunity to become established in a community and to meet people. We are always amazed at the number of people who are new to a community and who have little or no way of belonging. And, in this highly mobile society, there are probably many people who are new to your area. (This, of course, is less true in very small, rural communities. But, as we all know, many city slickers are escaping to the country. A lot of them feel some measure of guilt for their invasion and all of them feel like outsiders. You can take full advantage of this by recruiting them for your board.)

On the personal level, people are always looking for ways to meet other people. Being on a board of directors is a perfect opportunity. Presumably, all of the board members have *something* in common or they would not be interested in the agency. Some people are looking for friends or for business allies. Others are looking for someone to date.

Are we saying you should portray your agency as a singles club? Of course not. But you should point out to prospective candidates that some of the most interesting people in the area are members of your board.

    C. It will help anyone who wants to start his or her own nonprofit. At least once a week, someone will ask us how they should go about starting their own nonprofit agency. Our first and most important piece of advice is always "Join the board of a well-established agency in your community." It is the best way to get an excellent overview of everything that makes a nonprofit tick. They will also make invaluable contacts. And while this type of person usually has little or no experience in the business of being a board member, we have found them to be very hardworking, motivated and eager to learn.

D. Do you offer good board training? Travel opportunities? We are going to assume you conduct some kind of board training. If not, there are some superb training packages and programs geared especially toward nonprofits. Many of them are very reasonably priced or even free. We strongly encourage you to provide regular (at least once a year) training for your board.

Assuming that you do, brag about it to potential candidates. No doubt it is free to board members and it can be a very rewarding and educational experience for them.

If your agency is affiliated with a national association or working on a cause of national interest, your board members might attend conferences throughout the country. Almost all of the major groups hold at least an annual conference. The location is often changed to make it more convenient for a wider variety of affiliated agencies.

We have met many great board members who tell us these trips were one of the best things that had ever happened to them. They learned a lot and they had an opportunity to see a totally different part of the country. And, of course, they had fun.

E. Is your agency known as a mover and shaker? A pioneer? A powerful force for change? A model of high standards and ethical behavior in a day and age when so many people are disillusioned with government and traditional heros? By association, your board members will inherit your agency's reputation. They will be perceived in the same light and, assuming it is a *positive* light, they will be better off for it.

Don't be afraid to articulate and sell the culture and reputation (as well as the mission) of your agency. People like being associated with a good thing and they instinctively know it brings out their personal best.

****

Most board members of nonprofits do not receive a salary for their work. Potential candidates (especially those who have not sat on other boards) need to understand this up front. However, if your agency reimburses board members for mileage, child care costs or other expenses, be sure to tell them. Many agencies have lost some of their best prospects because someone forgot to tell them that their travel expenses would be reimbursed. These people had very low incomes and could not afford to come to the meetings without financial assistance.

These are only a few of the benefits you may have to offer a board member in addition to giving them the chance to do some real good for the community. Think about your agency; you may want to write down some of the things you feel would attract board members. Try to reduce them to a simple sentence or two that would be appropriate for your board recruitment brochure.

You might be think this sounds like a slick Madison Avenue sales promotion. Well, yes and no. Once again, we turn to the for-profit business world for some guidance.

There is nothing wrong with selling something if you have something worthwhile to sell. And, there is nothing wrong with learning from the professionals on how to sell. They say you need to identify your product (your mission statement and agency description) and target your market (the type of board member you want). Most important, you need to tell them the *benefits* of your product (what they will gain by being on your board).

The key, of course, is honesty. None of us appreciates false advertising when it comes to something we buy for ourselves and no one will appreciate false advertising in relation to your agency and board of directors. Don't tell them you are a kick-butt organization if you are actually very conservative in your approach. Don't tell them they will play an important decision-making role if you simply want a board that shows up four times a year for an hour and approves everything the director requests. Above all, never, ever misrepresent the mission of your agency.

The honesty must carry through in all communications with potential board members. Remember when Candy told Janice St. James that fund-raising was one of the weak links in the agency? Good move. First of all, it was true. Second of all, Janice knew exactly what she was getting herself into. In fact, Janice might not have been motivated to join the board if the agency already had a solid fund-raising campaign well underway. Third, as a new board member, Janice had immediate faith in Candy's integrity.

Just as we believe nonprofits should be run like businesses, so do we believe that marketing is an essential part of the business. You cannot expect to make it even in the nonprofit world without a solid marketing plan (of course, that extends to your funding sources, your clients and the community at

large). As long as you are honest, you are not being slick. You are just very good at what you do.

3. What do you expect from them?

This is another very important (and often overlooked) question. Let's start with the basics. How often does the board meet? How long are the average meetings? How long (in years) does a board member serve? Do you expect them to join board committees? Attend benefit dinners? Sign agency checks? Hold bake sales? Provide free professional advice?

Most people feel they do not have enough time and money. Although they get nervous if they sense you are trying to part them with their money, they get downright hostile if they think you are either wasting or taking up too much of their time. Be sure they know up front how much time you expect from them.

If you recruit a doctor, lawyer, accountant or other professional and you expect these people to donate

their services to the organization, you must absolutely tell them. It is one thing for them to enhance the
credibility of your board roster with their credentials.
It is another for them to provide their services free.
Some may be willing to do it *provided you have told
them up front this is what you want and need from
them.* (You will also need to be prepared to deal with
the liability issue. Unless you can cover them under
your agency's insurance, 99% of them will not even
consider donating their services.)

Finally, you must be careful not to take people for
granted by assuming they have a lot of free time.
Stay-at-home mothers (or fathers) and retired senior
citizens are often the victims of this unfair attitude.
People think simply because someone does not
work outside of the home or because they are
retired, he or she cannot be very busy. In fact, home
based parents and retired persons are extremely
busy people. Take this into consideration when you
lay out your expectations. Treat everyone as if they
were professionals and as if their time was extremely
valuable. Their time is just as important as the high-
powered business executive's time—and equally
precious to them!

Nothing will impress people more than if they feel
you are clear about what you want and need from
them and what you have to offer. Be honest, up front
and direct with them on these issues and you will
save yourself (and them) a lot of grief later on.

WHERE TO
FIND THEM:

It's easier than you think!

4

By this time, you have a done a lot of the work needed to figure out who should be on your board. Now let's talk about how and where to find them.

1. Right under your nose!

There are potential gold mines everywhere you turn in your daily life. Your hairdresser or barber, accountant, lawyer, priest, minister or rabbi, green grocer, tinker, tailor and so forth might be good candidates. Regardless of their profession, they have a vested interest in the community. If they are responsible, caring and thoughtful people, they could make excellent board members. All of us who have ever looked desperately for members have a tendency to take off our board recruiter hats when we go about our personal business. As a result, we often overlook some top-notch candidates.

There are, of course, some people who are right under (or next to) your nose that you should automatically exclude from consideration. Chief among these are family members. All nonprofits should have a nepotism clause prohibiting the agency from hiring staff members who are closely related to or in a close relationship with board members. Some prohibit anyone from serving on the board who is closely related to another board member.

Whether or not your agency has this type of provision in its charter documents (and if it doesn't, we strongly recommend that you adopt one), it is a very good idea to avoid such family ties. We have seen some ugly, unprofessional moments at board meetings when husbands and wives or sisters and brothers have used these public forums as the arenas for all of their personal differences. Equally as destructive, alliances are formed among these related board members based on blood, not on reason. It is not fair to anyone. Avoid these situations at all costs.

2. Advertise for them.
We are serious. Now, you probably won't want to take out a full page, four- color spread in the country's largest magazine, but you certainly could put a small notice in church bulletins or school and civic group newsletters. Many companies have employee newsletters. Because local businesses want (or feel it is in their best interests) to contribute to their communities, they should be very willing to let you put in a recruitment notice. We have even seen board recruitment ads in the classified section of newspapers. Why not?

3. Target the professional associations of those professions you really need.
Are you trying to get a certified public accountant on your board? Find the local association (state or national groups are less accessible) of accountants and approach the president. These

groups also have newsletters or they may be willing to let you give a brief presentation at their next luncheon, dinner or other function. Attorneys, physicians and others usually belong to one or more professional associations and these are ideal forums for recruitment.

4. Put the word out.

Who is the first person most likely to meet someone moving into the community? If you said the real estate agent, you get the prize. Most home buyers and even many renters consult real estate agents to help them get situated. Approach some of the realtors in your area. Tell them what your agency is about and ask them if they would pass out your brochure to newcomers. Remember, realtors are business people too. They want to show their support of community activities; helping out worthwhile nonprofits is a great way of doing it. And, as we said before, new people in town are always on the lookout for ways to belong.

You can call upon churches, the Better Business Bureau and civic groups for help. Ask them to keep you in mind and, if they spot someone who might be a good candidate for your board, to give that person one of your brochures.

5. Raid other boards.

Well, maybe "raid" is too strong a word. But you should make it your business to attend the board meetings of other nonprofits. (We think you should do this any way. Nonprofits must keep in close touch because among them, they make up a very important service network in the community. Even agencies with different purposes need to know what the others are doing and should be ready to form a coalition of agencies to address key issues of con- cern to everyone. Nothing will give you a better quick overview of an agency than its board meetings. But we are digressing again.) Except under extraordinary circumstances, board meetings are supposed to be advertised in advance and open to the public. Go to these meetings and see if there are some top notch board members you might be able to recruit for your agency.

Earlier in this guide, we said you should watch out for quasi-professional board members. We stand by that statement. However, we also said that being on the board of two (or more) different agencies might be beneficial for all concerned. If there is someone on another organization's board you think would be a good addition to your board, by all means you should approach them. He or she might turn you down or tell you they would be interested in serving on your board when their term with the other agency is done. This is common.

Many board members purposely don't let themselves get stale and like to switch agencies somewhere along the line. They may also be interested in different causes. Or, because most agency by-laws have a maximum number of cumulative years someone may serve as a board member, they may be going off the board in the near future and want to find another agency to work with. Finally, they might be ready, willing and able to serve on two boards at once. The point is you won't know until and unless you ask.

If they are not interested now, ask them to keep you in mind. Give them your brochure and your card. Be sure you know where to reach them for future refer-

ence. It doesn't hurt to check back with excellent prospects every so often. If you are not pushy, they will be flattered, not bugged.

Of course, you should not wait in the halls of other agencies like a vulture ready to pounce on unsuspecting, innocent board members. At the same time, don't be reluctant to approach someone just because he or she sits on another board.

6. Recruit your agency's clients.

You may not have a choice in this. As we said earlier, many programs (especially federally-funded ones) require that a certain number of your board members be representative of the people whom your agency serves. But, as we also said, you should really consider recruiting some of your agency's clients even if you have no such mandate from your funding source. We think this type of representation is an absolutely essential ingredient to any good board.

No one, especially your clients, should feel pressured to sit on your board. However, you may be pleasantly surprised at how many of your clients would love to become more involved. Develop a special brochure or flier especially for your "consumers" and make it available in your waiting room or lobby area. Leave copies in the waiting rooms of other agencies providing services to your clients as well.

7. Hold an open house or reception.
You may or may not want to hold such an event just for the purpose of recruiting board members. In fact, if that is your only purpose, you might not have a lot of people show up! However, if you have a new or renovated building, just received major funding for a new program initiative, want to say thank you to the community or even just celebrate the holiday season, use the opportunity to recruit new board members. Place some brochures and one of your best spokespersons near the goodies table (yes, you should spring for some munchies—it is the best way to draw people to anything) and have that person be prepared to schmooz.

The point is you should use every positive event as an opportunity to bring them in. We said it before—people like to be associated with a good thing. If you just got the big bucks to open up a clinic on the south side of town, celebrate the occasion and let potential board members celebrate with you. Half of the work (making them think this is a good, worthwhile and "happening" agency) has already been done for you.

8. Issue a news release about your agency.

A good write up in the local paper (maybe even a national one?) or a favorable two-minute spot on the evening news are invaluable marketing (recruitment) tools. Businesses in the for-profit world would kill for this free exposure. As a nonprofit, you are probably in the business of making the world a better place. That should make for more newsworthy press than selling widgets.

Don't expect them to run your story in the closing days of a major election or one the same day a hurricane is descending upon the city packing winds of 165 miles per hour. When the Berlin Wall came down and when the missiles were flying in Desert Storm, almost everyone in the world was watching. Local issues, even significant ones, paled in comparison. Look for a lull in the news and offer them something substantial. They will run your piece and you can get a lot of mileage out of it in many arenas, including board recruitment.

Another way to get noticed is to time your announcements to coincide with relevant events and holidays. If your state's governor has declared August 5th as Senior Citizen Day or October as Child Abuse Prevention Month and you run an agency serving senior citizens or abused children, you have a built in advantage. Use it. Call up the media and give them something they can use to fill out their coverage of these events.

If you have a cause without a designated day, week or month, all is not lost. Write your governor and tell him or her about the importance of your issue. We have seen gutsy board members do just that and get a day officially dedicated to their cause. They created the forum for themselves and made full use of it for some prime media coverage to recruit new board members. It helped their donation levels, too.

All good news releases and stories must grab the public on several levels. First, your agency's mission should come shining through. Second, the community should be able to relate to what you are saying. Make it relevant to the important local issues of the day. Third, your agency must stand out from the others. This does not mean you should put anyone else down. However, you want to be *the* magnet for people who are interested in this particular cause.

Start off with the most important information first. If they are going to chop the news release, they will cut off the end, not the beginning. In the last section of this guide, we have a sample news release you may use for your own agency.

9. Get a booth at local fairs, conferences or charity events.

Once again, the primary *stated* purpose of having a booth would not be to recruit board members. You would want to have brochures about your agency's programs and services. Get some good pictures of your staff in action and have them made into posters to make your booth more attractive and exciting.

You can place your board recruitment brochure along side your program write-ups. If possible, get your best board members to man (or woman) the booth at key times to answer questions. Be sure everyone who answers questions about the agency, including questions about the board of directors, has been coached to give consistent and good answers.

Finding Them Include a poster that looks like a classy invitation cordially inviting them to the next board meeting. List the date, time and location. Offer refreshments. (Except for money, little else draws people, any kind of people, like free food. Accept this as a fact of life and use it to your advantage.)

Regardless of the event, try to get a centrally located booth so you get a lot of "foot traffic." Have plenty of materials on hand.

Offer something special to pull them in. At a state fair several years ago, one nonprofit agency attracted hundreds of people by offering to fingerprint their children on police department approved cards. (The agency provides child-related services.) Parents were given the cards to keep in the unthinkable event that one of their children was missing. As the children were being finger printed, agency staff and board members took the opportunity to tell the parents all about the agency and to mention (casually, of course) the board openings. It was an extremely clever, relevant and appropriate way to attract interest and it worked.

Decorate helium filled balloons or tee-shirts with your agency's name and logo. (By the way, get a good logo if your agency doesn't already have one!) Or, if balloons and tee-shirts are not available, try posters, bumper stickers, pens or mugs. Some of these cost more than others, of course, but you might be able to get a shop in town to donate them. Use them to publicize your agency, raise funds *and* to recruit board members.

In our experience, booths at fairs, conferences or other community functions are one of the best ways

to recruit board members. Take a look at what is going on in your community and see if you can make these events work for you.

10. Take advantage of public service announcements, community calendars and other free advertising.

Local television and radio stations must donate air time to community events and public causes. Most of them are very glad to do so. Get the names of the contact people in each of the local channels or stations and ask them to run announcements for you. Remember, there are many other agencies who want to use this valuable resource as well, so be sure to give them plenty of lead time and don't abuse the privilege.

Write a thirty and a sixty-second spot. Keep them simple but snappy. Practice reading them aloud to see if they sound good. And don't forget to include the agency's name and phone number!

11. Hold a workshop or a conference related to your agency's cause and invite some potential board members. Include a board recruitment brochure in the registration packets of everyone who attends the conference.

A good workshop or conference is one of the best ways in the world to educate people about your agency's mission. It then becomes an ideal platform for recruitment of board members. Again, the organization and its work are the focus of the conference. However, you should take full advantage of the situation to approach some potential candidates for your board.

12. Recruit professors and instructors at nearby colleges, universities and other institutions of higher learning.

People in academics are forever accused of living in an ivory tower. For those involved in the social sciences, this accusation can be particularly damaging because their specialties almost always mandate a hands-on involvement with the world around them. Being on the board of a nonprofit agency dedicated to the field or discipline in which they have specialized is a great way to combat this negative perception. It can also help them advance in their academic standing and give their publications (something every academic must have) even more credibility.

Try to match your agency with professors and instructors who teach subjects related to your organization's cause. For example, a professor in early-child development would be great to have on the board of a nonprofit day-care center. A professor in the Department of Social Work could be an outstanding member of a board for an agency devoted to case management and services for seniors. An economist would be appropriate for an ecomonic development corporation.

13. Do you know any celebrities? Real ones? Get them to help you.

If you know any bona fide celebrities (or know someone who knows a celebrity well) ask them to be at least an honorary member of your board. They probably won't have the time to sit in on all (or even most) board meetings. But even if they appear once a year or every other year, you have a gold mine. If your agency's letterhead lists all of its board members on the top or side (something you might consider if you have a board with relatively little turnover) ask the celebrity if it would be all right to list his or her name as an honorary member.

If the superstar feels uncomfortable being a board member, even an honorary one, see if he or she will make an appearance at your annual dinner or some other special agency function. Ask them to give a brief talk about the organization and its cause and to help you recruit new board members.

Celebrities are overwhelmed with requests for money and help. Everyone wants a piece of the magic they bring. Be aware of this when you make your presentation. Be succinct and professional (in other words, try not to be star-struck) and be sure the celebrity is at least sympathetic to your cause!

****

Finding Them These are only some of the ways you can locate good potential board members. Undoubtedly you will think of others that will work for your particular agency and situation. The key is to examine every possible encounter with candidates and to make the most out of it. And while this does *not* mean you should leap out from darkened doorways at strangers walking down the street, fall to your knees and beg them to sit on your board, it *does* mean you should be prepared to answer questions about your agency if a good prospect appears interested.

THE DO'S AND DON'TS OF BOARD RECRUITMENT:

How to get them to join your board

5

O.K! So far you have taken stock of the agency and you know what you need in terms of talents, characteristics and personalities. We also discussed different places and ways to find good candidates. Now it is time to talk about the specific things you can do to make them join your board. We will also talk about some of the things you absolutely should not do. Most of these are simply common sense.

We already began our discussion of the do's and don'ts when we sat in on Jim Smith and Candy Altura's respective recruitment meetings. Let's pick up from there.

1. Size up your candidate and pitch your recruitment efforts accordingly.

Remember when Candy asked Janice St. James what she did at the XYZ Foundation? When Janice said she was the fund raiser, Candy responded appropriately and geared the discussion toward Janice's stated interest. It worked. By the end of the meeting, Janice was clearly hooked.

Conversely, Jim seemed completely oblivious to Bob's profession. Don't make this mistake! If you are dealing with an accountant, highlight your concern for use of funds and sound fiscal practices. If you are trying to recruit a social worker, discuss your concern for the clients' right to dignity. If you have one of your agency's clients sitting in front of you, talk about the compelling need for client input.

It bears repeating—we assume you have a good product (your agency and its mission) and that you are prepared to sell this product honestly. But that does not preclude you from establishing some common ground with each person you are trying to recruit.

2. Don't presume and don't assume.

We don't mean to keep picking on poor James, but he made two other mistakes almost immediately. First, he began by calling Bob by his first name. While some people don't mind this sort of casual, informal approach, others find it very presumptuous. Candy did not make this mistake.

Younger or older, it is always wise to address people you have just met by Mr., Mrs., Ms., Doctor or whatever title is appropriate. If they ask you to call them by their first name, go ahead and do so. However, if Ms. McLandon says you may call her Deborah, do not call her Debbie! Above all, never, ever (we say again, never) refer to men as Mr.-So-and-So and women by their first names. We still see it happen a lot. In this day and age, you could be shot at dawn and, quite frankly, you would deserve it.

The second thing Jim did was to assume Bob was already committed to joining the board. *"I am glad you have decided to join our agency's board."* Ob- viously, Bob had not already decided to join.

Even if he had, however, everyone likes to be courted and no one likes to be taken for granted. Don't assume you have someone committed to your board until the person has actually said yes. Then be sure to thank them.

3. Be prepared to negotiate.

There will be people who can make a valuable contribution to your agency but who simply cannot commit themselves to everything you want and need. And while you must have a bottom line (for example, if there are twelve meetings a year, you probably cannot accommodate someone who can make less than half of them), it will be in your best interests to be as flexible as you can. It will also make the person feel important which never hurts.

Once you strike a deal, however, you have every right to expect the person to hold up his or her end of the bargain. If they say they can only make every other meeting and you agree, fine. If they only show up once a year (coincidentally when the agency has its open house during the holiday season) that is not so fine and these people should probably not be on the board.

4. Put your best foot forward.

How does this relate to board recruitment? Make sure your best spokespersons (be they executive staff or board members) conduct the board recruitment. They should be clear, direct and have a very good idea of what the agency is all about. These spokespersons don't have to be geniuses or extremely sophisticated—but they do have to know how to handle themselves and how to answer questions. They should be enthusiastic about the agency and its mission. Frankly, James Smith should not have been the one talking to Robert Jones.

Not everyone is good at this type of thing. In fact, maybe you are not, either. That's ok and no one should get their feelings hurt. Undoubtedly they (or you) have other skills and gifts that are very important to the agency. The trick is to know who would be appropriate and to use their skills.

Finally, every organization has a fluffhead, a chatterbox or a grouch. He or she may have a heart of gold and could be among the agency's most loyal board members. They never miss a board meeting and they have always come through when envelopes need to be stuffed or when someone has to dress up as Santa Claus for the children's Christmas party at the local hospital. Treasure and respect them for what they have to offer, but don't make (or let) them be the ones to recruit other board members.

5. Invite the potential candidates to a board meeting and conduct a very good meeting.
This is the place where they will see you (both the board and executive staff) in action. A well run meeting with an action-packed, meaningful agenda is very impressive. A poorly run meeting is a nightmare.

One word of caution. A well run meeting is not synonymous with marine boot camp. Don't be a dictator! Let people express their opinions and let them have fun. Just don't let them wander all over the place—literally or figuratively.

It is also important to make sure everyone is on their best behavior. We once witnessed a serious food fight break out among board members of a nonprofit after someone made a very rude remark. We must be honest: For us, it was absolutely one of the funniest things we have ever seen. Not so for the potential board members who had been invited to the meeting to observe the agency in action. As chili dogs and french fries flew through the air, they quietly slipped out the back door.

The food fight was, blessedly, an extreme case. However, there are many times when bickering among board members and/or executive staff erupts into open warfare. Do not, under any circumstance, let this happen on any scale.

6. Invite them to tour the agency during working hours. Make sure the staff knows that potential

board members will be visiting.

Again, the conduct of everyone involved will make or break this encounter. An enthusiastic atmosphere is contagious and any potential board member who is remotely interested in what the agency does will be hooked. On the other hand, if your staff just sits around moping and watching the clock . . .

Every work place, whether it is a shoe lace factory or a nonprofit working with teens, has its own atmosphere or what we call its culture. Good agencies have dynamic cultures—you can feel it the minute you hit the door. Look at the culture of your agency and see if it could be a strong selling point for potential board members.

7. Don't pressure them and never put a guilt trip on them.

This may sound like a contradiction after we have been advising you to "sell" board members on your organization. Not really. It is one thing to give it your best shot—it is another thing to badger them or to make them feel guilty about not joining.

Anyone who has been in the situation of recruiting board members (and we are no exception) has engaged in "guilting" people to some degree. You get desperate and you need to fill out that board roster! In the end, however, it is not worth it. They will not come through for you because their heart was not in it in the first place. They just said yes because they did not know how to turn you down.

If you feel someone is really reluctant to join, back off. Give him or her a copy of your brochure and your card and ask them to call you if they ever change their mind.

8. Take the fear and mystery out of the phrase "board of directors" for those people who have never belonged to a board before.

A lot of people have a preconceived notion of what a board of directors is. It sounds very formal and business like. Inviting them to attend a board meeting (remember, we said it should be fun, too!) is one of the best ways to take the mystique out of the whole thing.

You might also consider an orientation session for prospective candidates. During this session, which should be informal, give them some of the basic information they will need to know so they feel they will be able to navigate their way around in this strange new world.

Many board training packages can easily be adapted to a pre-board session. Some of your experienced (and articulate, remember?) board members may be interested in developing a two or three-hour package on "Everything you wanted to know about being on a board but were afraid to ask." Keep it fun and focused.

9. Give them alternate ways to make a contribution to the agency.

Perhaps they are not ready to take the plunge and become a board member right now. But if they believe in what your organization is doing, they may be willing to help out in another capacity.

If your agency is like most, you can use all of the help you can get. And some of the best board members we know started in a less formal capacity. Once they became familiar with the agency, they decided they were ready to sit on the board.

Later on, we will discuss some of the things these people can do to help you without joining the board. The possibilities are almost endless.

10. Be completely honest with your board members and candidates.

It is easy to, well, gloss over the truth. But potential board members should know the responsibilities and potential liabilities they will have. You don't need to scare the pants off them. However, being on a board does make one responsible for what happens in the agency and they have every right to know that.

On the other hand, don't give them any illusions of grandeur. We sat in on one board orientation session in which the recruiter made it seem as if the board members would be ruling a kingdom. "You will have a private office in the agency," she said. "You will have a secretary at your beck and call." Not good.

First, in all of our experience, we have seen only two agencies in which an office set aside solely for board members' use was appropriate (because of the unique circumstances of these agencies at that point in time). We have never seen a nonprofit agency in which there was enough staff to have a secretary at the beck and call of anybody, let alone a board member.

Second, the recruiter was painting a false picture of life as a board member. She had accurately read the audience and knew they would like these trappings of power. But it was completely inappropriate. Two people in the audience did join the agency's board (for all of the wrong reasons, of course) and had a rude awakening when their private offices did not

materialize and no one was waiting to do their every bidding.

You must also be completely honest about the organization. If your agency has some weaknesses and a potential board member asks you about them, answer the questions directly. Remember Candy's discussion with Janice St. James? No one expects a perfect agency. In fact, some of the best possible candidates, like Janice, need a good challenge and would love to take a weakness and turn it into an agency strength.

11. Be aware of the impression that your board members make.

This goes for their conduct during meetings as well as their conduct in general. We don't mean you should try to get all of your board members to adhere to your personal vision of a "proper" lifestyle. Of course you shouldn't and your board members would resent it terribly. However, if half of your board has been arrested for drunk driving or several board members are known for writing bad checks at every store in town, your agency's reputation will suffer. So will your recruitment efforts.

Your by-laws should have something about the kind of conduct expected from board members. Again, you must separate inappropriate conduct from different ways of thinking and living. Once you have done that, however, you should expect your board members to behave themselves if they want to stay on the board.

WHAT TO DO IF YOU HAVE NO CHOICE:

How to deal with board members
others have selected for you

6

Throughout this guide, we have concentrated on active recruitment strategies—that is, you have figured out the board members you need and how to get them. But many nonprofits are bound by laws, regulations or guidelines that require someone else to do the selection of at least some of the agency's board members. For example, one type of agency is required by federal law to have elected officials or their designees sit on their boards. These agencies have absolutely no choice in who is elected or, if the official chooses not to serve on the board, whom he or she designates to sit on the board in his or her stead.

Here is another area in which we have extremely mixed feelings. On one hand, this outside input keeps an agency from becoming totally self-contained. Often, agencies with boards having complete and total discretion over the selection of all of the members become stale or, even worse, self-serving. The community served by the agency is left out in the cold.

This board selection process forces the community to take some responsibility for the agency. The community must come up with at least some of the board members for the agency and its mission.

On the other hand, it is easier to walk barefoot over hot coals or lie on a bed of nails (we really are not exaggerating that much) than to put up with some of the board members we have known who have been appointed by outside entities. Please understand; not all of these appointees are board members from hell. Some of them are very good and make excellent contributions to the agencies. However, some of them are known in their communities as living nightmares. They are disruptive, uncooperative, ignorant and pompous.

Depending upon your agency's funding source re- quirements and other rules and regulations, there may be very little you can do to change the way in which members are seated on your board. And, as we said before, there are many advantages to having someone else be responsible for finding at least some of your board members.

In the previous section, we noted that you can set the ground rules for conduct, attendance, responsibilities and participation. If these ground rules are violated, you have every right to remove such people from your board. There are several ways of doing this.

The easiest way, if they are agreeable, is to get these individuals to resign. Be diplomatic but direct. "Perhaps you didn't realize the kind of commitment being on this board would take," you might say. "You don't seem to enjoy attending the board meetings. You also don't seem to have the time to take on any additional projects. Maybe you would like to resign. We would be more than happy to consider you again as a board member in the future if you find you have more time."

We have used lines like that ourselves and they usually work.

If the person resists taking the hint, doesn't change his or her behavior and doesn't resign, the second easiest way is to speak, if applicable, to the official who put the blockhead on the board in the first place. For example, if your by-laws call for a representative from the mayor's office and the mayor appoints a real loser (who refuses to step down) you might approach the mayor directly.

"Your Honor, I know you are far too busy to sit on our board yourself. However, I would really appreciate it if you would reconsider your appointment of Ms. Norris. To be frank, she does not convey the impression that I think you would want. We have had a lot of media attention these days because of the new clinic and, well, she doesn't adequately represent your role in all of this. Perhaps there is someone in your office who is more sensitive to the situation and your viewpoint."

That is exactly what we said to one mayor. Notice what we stressed. Acknowledgement of how busy the mayor was. The mayor's image as represented by Ms. Norris. The media. Giving the mayor credit for the clinic. Getting someone more like the mayor. This, too, worked.

(By the way, if the mayor to whom this was addressed, or any other mayor or official reads this and thinks it was manipulative, we make no apologies. We only use these tactics when confronted with really impossible board members. Please think about this if you are asked to appoint board members to that community nonprofit!)

If neither of these tactics work, it is time to get tough. Assuming your by-laws have good, solid and objective criteria governing what board members must do, you should enforce these provisions. If the board member in question (however he got there) doesn't measure up to these requirements, remove him.

Is there a provision for excused and unexcused absences in the by-laws? Have the board members had more than the allowable number of unexcused absences? Have they failed to participate in required standing committees? Have they conducted them- selves inappropriately at board meetings? Have they violated the agency's strict client confidentiality requirements?

The key, as we said before, is objective criteria. Appropriate or inappropriate conduct is the most subjective of all of those we listed, but beyond a certain point, that, too, becomes obvious enough to warrant taking action.

By trying to talk to the person himself and, if applicable, going to the person who appointed him, you have also covered your bases. If you get to the point where you need to take action to remove him, no one can say they were not aware of the problem.

Now, for some hard, cold reality. There are times when you simply cannot get someone off of your board. Perhaps, as damaging as they are, they have done nothing to violate your by-laws. Perhaps (and this is a common scenario) the mayor is trying to find something for his deadbeat staff member to do to keep him or her out of his honor's hair. Or, perhaps the mayor thinks the staff person walks on water and has no idea why you are raising any concerns.

If you find there is no proper way to get the person off of the board, accept it and work around him. Don't, in the middle of such a controversy, amend your by-laws simply to take care of the immediate situation. Don't try to hold meetings without the jerk. Don't slash his tires or send him anonymous death threats.

All of these are very tempting thoughts. Again, from personal experience, we know! In our minds, we have concocted many elaborate schemes to avoid dealing with the board member from hell. In the end, however, reason prevailed.

In these situations, it is up to your board president or chairperson to conduct the board meetings in such a way as to minimize the damage. Having a good, tight agenda, sticking to it, effectively cutting off unproductive discourses and exchanges, knowing and implementing Robert's Rules of Order (or whatever parliamentary procedures your board has adopted)—all of these are tools and techniques that a good chairperson can use. They work.

So, you ask, what do you do if the board member from hell is the chairperson? Well, then, like the author of this book, you too probably pulled the wings off helpless insects in your previous life . . .

Remember: There is a great deal of difference between board members who are feisty, opinionated, crusty, stubborn, sometimes difficult (or whatever it is that might bug you) and board members who really don't belong there at all. Please don't ever try to remove someone just because they rub you (or others) the wrong way or because they look at things differently than you do.

HOW TO HOLD ONTO GOOD BOARD MEMBERS ONCE YOU HAVE THEM:

Strategies for keeping them
around for a long time

7

Getting good board members is only half of the story (or, if you prefer, battle). Now you have to keep them! Only if they stay on your board for a number of years can they make the kind of contributions you need. And, a high board vacancy rate means you will be spending a good deal of your time recruiting new members. Even with this guide in hand, we would hate to think of you spending all of your waking hours looking for good candidates.

The do's and don'ts from the earlier chapter apply here as well. Continue to show them the respect they deserve (even if you become very friendly with them) and never take them for granted. Always be prepared to answer their questions. Don't tell them half truths.

There are many other strategies you can use to guarantee your board members will be around for more than a couple of board meetings. While we hope these strategies are part of your normal way of doing business, they are worth stating. All of us, even the most considerate people in the world, get busy and stressed. In those moments, we tend to let some things get by us.

1. Come through with the "benefits" you promised during the recruitment.

If you told them they will have the opportunity to represent the agency at the upcoming national conference in Los Angeles, send them to Los Angeles unless there is a very good and compelling reason not to do so.

2. If you are an executive staff member or the chairperson of the board, always prepare for board meetings and always get yourself psyched for a good meeting.

Sometimes this is hard. We know! Board meetings can be tedious (especially if you have already done them a thousand times before) and there are times when you think you just can't get revved up for another one. When we felt that way, we would think of the Broadway musical stars who must go out there, night after night and (if the show is a hit) even year after year. Every time, they have to be as enthusiastic as they were on opening night. It is extremely difficult but that is one of the qualities separating the professionals from the amateurs. Same thing here.

The time you invest in preparation for board meetings and the time you put into delivering a top quality board meeting is never wasted—not just in keeping your good board members, but also in establishing and maintaining long-term credibility.

3. Treat board meetings like the business meetings they really are.

Remember: a nonprofit is a business and the board meetings are where the policy decisions for the business are made. They are important and the way in which you conduct yourself at these meetings will have far reaching ramifications.

Don't misunderstand: we are not saying you need to get out your dark blue suit and act as if you are making a major presentation on Wall Street. If your agency has a casual atmosphere, your board meetings are likely to be casual as well. But casual should not mean unprofessional.

4. Try not to load down the good board members with all of the work.

That, too, is hard advice to follow. In every agency, there are always the workhorses on the staff and board who do almost everything. You know they will come through and so you tend to give them anything of consequence that needs to be done. All of us do this.

Hold onto Them! In our interviews with board members, we found this to be the number one reason the good ones resigned from boards. They were overwhelmed with projects while other board members literally just sat there or didn't even bother showing up at all. It is just too discouraging and time consuming. As one excellent board member told us, "It is bad enough that I have to work around the deadbeats in my office. At least I get paid there. But to go through the same thing as a volunteer board member is adding insult to injury."

So, you say, how do you keep that from happening? By doing everything in your power to get as many board members as you can who are prepared to share the work equally. As we said before, let people know up front what you expect of them. It may take you a while, but you will gradually have a board filled with productive members. They will set the standard for anyone else who joins.

5. Maintain contact with them between meetings.

This is especially important if you have infrequent (fewer than 8 a year) board meetings. If the only time they ever see you and the agency is during a board meeting once every three months, they simply won't be as invested in the agency. You must be a large (but not burdensome) part of their lives.

A good way to do this is to call them up every once in a while. Was there a key point that board member Ray Allen wanted you to follow up on at the last meeting? Don't wait for the next one to let him know what you found out. Research it quickly and get back to him. Of course, you will go over the issue at the next meeting, but by that time Mr. Allen will know all about it because you already told him.

6. Keep them informed of what is happening.

You should always be sure your board members, especially your key ones, are up-to-date on the latest events. That goes for the good stuff as well as the bad. During your telephone conversations, fill them in. Don't let them read about an agency crisis or triumph in the newspaper without having heard it from you first. It will make them feel foolish and embarrassed.

There is no need to spend hours going over every little detail. Stick to the important stuff. We know one executive director who felt it was essential to tell her board chairman everything. Literally everything.

"The postman is late again," she would say. "The plumber just came to fix the staff toilet." The poor chairman got at least four calls a day chronicling the saga of the exterminator, the adventures of the painter, the routine correspondence from the funding sources . . . he heard it all. He was a very patient (too patient) man, but even he had his limits. He resigned quite suddenly one day in the middle of a detailed report on the deterioration of the quality of number 2 lead pencils.

7. Give credit where credit is due.

If one of your board members helped to negotiate a great lease arrangement for the organization, make sure everyone knows that. You don't have to go overboard, but be sure the other board members and staff are aware that board treasurer Sandra Sanchez was the one who convinced Arlen Covey to reduce his rent by almost a third. If you have an agency newsletter, be sure to acknowledge board contributions as well as recognizing staff achievements.

8. Give them the best board training you can afford.

Nothing pulls a board together or reinforces existing bonds like a good training session. Look around in your community for a great board trainer. Check the United Way, other established nonprofits, the university and private consultants. Make sure the training is relevant to your agency. Stay away from "canned" presentations.

Because many of your board members work during the day, you may need to hold these sessions on a Saturday. All the more reason you want the training to be as good as it can be—you are asking them to give up more of their time. But a top-notch training session will work wonders.

If you have a large number of new board members, consider a basic training and orientation package to get them started. This will help them feel they are on equal footing with the other, more experienced board members and it will let them know they are important to you.

We highly recommend training at least on an annual basis. It might be coupled with a board retreat (different from training, a board retreat typically helps members assess where the agency has been and where it should go) at the annual meeting. Never assume your board members know everything there is to know about the agency and never pass up this golden opportunity to make your board feel good about its role and its commitment to the agency.

9. Try not to get involved in board cliques.

At one time or another in the life of an agency, there are bound to be different "camps" of board

members. It seems inevitable. Sometimes the staff is pulled into these different camps. As a board member or executive staff person, you will find you are more sympathetic to one group as opposed to the other.

As difficult as it is, try to stay out of any camps or cliques—even if you find you are more comfortable with one group than another. Why? Because you will unnecessarily alienate some of your board members and you must always try to remain objective. And, on a purely practical level, you do not want to burn your bridges unless you absolutely have no choice. You never know when you will need the support of those three naysayers who are always out to find fault with the agency's operations.

10. Try hard not to get involved on an extremely personal level with the other board members—at

75

least while both of you are serving on the board (or staff).

More difficult advice to follow! When two people are very attracted to each other (as friends or lovers) it is hard for them to stay apart. That is human nature and as we said earlier, meeting people is one of the chief reasons people join boards. But it does complicate business relationships and, at the risk of being repetitious, a nonprofit is a business. If you find yourself getting involved with someone else on the board or staff, you must do everything in your power to separate the personal relationship from the business of the agency. If you can't, then someone has to go.

11. Assess and re-assess the agency's goals on a regular basis.

Board retreats, as we noted earlier, are very important. Everyone gets so busy doing things that the reasons behind all of these activities may get lost. We all need to be reminded of our purpose, whether it be in our private lives, our jobs or in a nonprofit agency. Board members are no exception.

Take stock periodically of where the agency has been and where it is going. Implicit in this kind of exercise is a recognition of the contributions everyone (including board members) has made. Remind the board of the importance of their hard work and efforts.

We have found that a "big" retreat (as in a daylong session, preferably away from the agency and preferably led by an outside expert who knows how to facilitate group discussions) held once a year and a much more informal session at the six-month mark works very well. During the retreat, the agency's mission statement is re-examined, the goals are evaluated and progress is measured. With skillful guidance, these retreats will recharge everyone's batteries, re-establish unity and set the stage for the upcoming year. They can also be a lot of fun.

At the informal session, a brief summary of the progress during the last six months, followed by a discussion of any major issues is really all you need. The chairperson, other board member or executive director should be able to lead these sessions and they should take no longer than two hours max.

Don't overdo it. We know of agencies that put their board members through frequent soul-searching and bonding sessions ad nauseam in the name of agency unity and goal setting. "If I needed therapy, I would go see a shrink," said one board member we interviewed. "We never get anything done—we just sit around, talk about why we are here and congratulate ourselves and each other for being such caring people."

The point is we all need to stand back every once in a while and to reflect on why we do what we do. A nonprofit board of directors is no exception. However, if all the board does is talk—well, then you have a problem.

12. Listen to what they have to say.

These people joined your board because they care. They have important things to contribute to the agency and its direction.

People can always tell when someone they are talking to is not hearing a thing they are saying. Always give your board members your full attention.

Hold onto Them! If you have board members who go on and on and on, find a tactful way to end the conversation. But while you are talking to them, be sure your thoughts are not a thousand miles away.

All of these principles make sense and most are not hard to follow. You are simply treating people (in this case, the board members) the way you would want them to treat you. But these guidelines will serve you in good stead in the long run. We have talked to many ex-board members whose reasons for resigning from a board related to one or more of these issues.

Inevitably, you will have people resign for reasons that are beyond your control. They may move, they may become uncomfortable with the agency's direction or they may find themselves overextended. But, if you effectively address the issues you *can* control, you stand a much better chance of building a strong, stable board.

OTHER WAYS PEOPLE CAN HELP YOU WITHOUT JOINING YOUR BOARD:

Projects and ideas to suggest to them

8

Let's face it—despite all of your best efforts, some people simply don't want to be on your board. These people fall into two groups. The first is those people who, for whatever reason, don't want to be involved with your agency—at least not now. They may be too busy or they may not like what they saw or heard.

If someone is reluctant, back off. Don't try to guilt them into joining the board. They won't last. If they tell you they like your agency but just cannot be involved right now, keep their names, addresses and phone numbers on file. Send them a flyer or nice letter in about six months or a year. In the follow up letter, invite them to a board meeting or to call you if they are interested.

If you get the sense they were turned off for some reason, try, discreetly, to find out why. Again, marketing experts say you should always pay attention to the response you get from your advertising messages and change them if you get negative (or lukewarm) responses.

Above all, don't take it personally. Most people fear rejection, but the most successful get rejected all of the time. The trick is they keep on trying. Board recruitment is important stuff, but it is not a matter of life or death. All anyone can do is say no.

A negative answer is not going to cause the roof to cave in (literally or figuratively) and it doesn't mean you are a failure. If you need to identify some new techniques (like our old friend Jim), then learn them and promise yourself you will do better next time.

That, of course, was a pep talk, but we mean it!

Now, for the second group. You will come across many wonderful people who are not prepared to become board members. The title itself may scare them and, despite your efforts to reassure them, they may feel it is a formal, alien world.

If, after attending a board meeting and talking to other board members, they are still reluctant to join, don't pressure them. Instead, think of other ways they may want to help your agency and approach them on it. You might want to have what we call "The Plan B" brochure ready to give them listing other things they can do. (We have included a sample in the last section of the guide for you to use.)

If your agency is like most, some of the most important ways they can probably help are:

1. Volunteers: The entire infrastructure of nonprofit agency services would collapse tomorrow morning if it were not for the volunteers who answer phones, greet clients, stuff envelopes, make meals, transport clients, whatever. And that is no exaggeration. The funding received by all nonprofits does not begin to support all of the staff they need; volunteers make up the rest.

They don't have to put in a lot of time—especially at first. Ask them to consider even four hours a month. If they like it, they can increase the time. (Depending upon what volunteers in your agency do, you should give them an orientation session or training program. Tell them that when you approach them to be a volunteer so they know they will be prepared for whatever task they are going to take on.)

We know many good board members who chose to start as volunteers. It gave them the opportunity to see the agency from the inside. In fact, we think it made them better board members in the long run. Even if they don't ever "graduate" to being board members, however, you have an invaluable resource.

By the way, many funding sources (federal, state and even private) look at volunteer hours as a measure of community commitment to the agency. If an agency match is required (contributions from the agency used to match the money from the funding source), volunteer hours can frequently be used as an "in-kind" (non-cash) donation. Not only do you get the value of the volunteer's time, it can help you secure additional funds.

2. Fund Raiser: If you run into people who have a knack for organizing fund-raising events or approaching businesses, wealthy people or foundations for money, perhaps they will consider helping your agency. Ask them to coordinate a fund-raising campaign, a raffle, a benefit dinner or a bake sale. This

can be a one-time-only event which means they
don't have to commit themselves to the agency over
an extended period. Let's face it. Many people don't
like long-term commitments but would be very willing
to help you out on a short-term project.

3. Grassroots Supporter: Every nonprofit in the
world can use all of the support it can get from its
community. Even the best of them come up against
resistance from somebody at some point. They will
need people to show up at hearings, write letters to
the editor, talk to their neighbors—whatever. Don't
pass up the opportunity to cultivate anyone who can
do nothing more for your agency than to be there
when you need them to set the record straight.

You could designate a special name for these sup-
porters, such as "Friends of Centerville Senior
Agency," or something catchy like that. This title is
often used for people who donate money to an

agency. However, you are really asking them to be nothing more than what the title says—friends. They don't have to give any money. They only need to give a little bit of their time for special purposes. Send them a regular letter to keep them posted on the agency's activities. Let them know of key events (hearings, a request for a zoning variance, presentation before the City Council, whatever) and ask them to attend.

The fact that these people are not directly connected to your agency can actually work for you. Bureaucrats, officials and politicians frequently look at pleas from staff and board members with skepticism— they perceive these pitches for funding or special consideration as self-serving. But, if you have a bunch of people who attend the hearing and say "I am in no way connected with Centerville Senior Agency. However, I am a concerned citizen and I want to offer my support for their request . . . " you will see an entirely different kind of reaction.

4. Lobbyist: We aren't talking about the kind of paid lobbyist we associate with big business. We mean the kind of person who writes letters to their senator, representatives, the mayor, the president—anyone who needs to be reached. These lobbyists also testify at legislative hearings.

Lobbying activities are in the same vein as grassroots support but on a more general level. Lobbying for nonprofits usually means lobbying for their causes. In order to help get more funds for the senior service agency in their town, these lobbyists must convince state legislatures and the U.S. Congress that more funds should be appropriated for senior programs in general.

Regardless of the arena, anyone who lobbies has to know the facts and be prepared to state them clearly and succinctly. He or she will discuss the importance of the cause or service on a national as well as the local level. It takes a special kind of skill to be an effective lobbyist.

If the people you were recruiting to be board members are reluctant to sit on the board but have an excellent grasp of the issues related to your agency, perhaps they would be willing to lobby for you.

Writing letters is one thing they can do with little trouble. Make sure they have the latest facts and that they know what key legislation is pending before Congress or your state legislature.

If they will testify for your cause in front of state or federal legislative bodies, you are truly blessed among all mortals. Make sure they are prepared and can speak to the issue on the general as well as specific fronts.

There are several reasons why it is very effective to pull in outsiders to make these presentations. First, they don't have to be the only ones stating your case.

You and your board members can certainly write letters and make presentations as well. However, there are very strict guidelines for lobbying using public funds (federal, state and local tax dollars). If your salary is paid for with public dollars, you have to be extremely careful about engaging in anything that can be remotely construed as lobbying. While your board members are not paid salaries, they may have their travel expenses reimbursed with agency (and therefore public) dollars.

Second, as we mentioned in the discussion of grassroots support, legislators listen to people who are completely disassociated with a particular agency. Excellent and moving testimony from staff or board members is often discredited because many legislators think these people are only looking after their own interests.

Third, the more diverse and strong the support you can demonstrate, the more your cause will be taken seriously. If you have the banker (the one who can't sit on your board right now but who is extremely interested in what your agency does) up there testifying next to your board member followed by a group of clients and all of them are saying that funds for senior care programs must be increased, you have some real fire power.

5. Everyone (and everything!) Else: What would you do if we said seven people would be at the front door of your agency next Saturday morning and they were going to paint the place from top to bottom—all at no charge to you? Well, if you are in a beautiful, new, freshly painted building with gorgeous, deep-pile wall-to-wall carpeting, the thought would probably make you puke. However, if you are in an older, shabby, kind-of-run-down place, you would be delighted. There are a lot of people who would love to help out on a one-time-only basis. Painting a building (like the old-fashioned barn raising) is the kind of community project many people adore. There is instant gratification and a sense that they will make a lasting contribution.

Figure out what you need and see who is willing to do it. Room dividers? The furniture completely rearranged to make best use of your limited space? Cleaning out that old storeroom with records and files dating back to 1965? Sometimes outsiders will approach this kind of task with an enthusiasm the staff just can't muster up. As a result, they actually do a much better job.

The sculptor who will make and donate a special piece for your waiting area, the artist who will design a new logo, the pastry chef who will provide a fabulous dessert to go with the coffee at the annual meeting—all of these people can contribute in ways other than being on your board. It is up to you to sense where they are coming from and to offer them alternate ways to contribute.

6. Go for the green: We would be remiss if we did not mention one of the most basic contributions of all—money. It would not be appropriate for you to approach all of the people who turned down your invitation to sit on the board for cash. For example, you would never approach your clients—especially if they are low-income—for money. However, if you asked the manager at the local (and thriving) car dealership to sit on your board and he said, "Well, you know, I really think you are doing a great job over there but I just don't have the time right now . . ." you should respond with, "Well, I can certainly understand that. I see how many cars you sell here. It must keep you really hopping. Perhaps, instead, you would be willing to make the first donation toward the new wing on our day-care center? Or donate a car for us to raffle off?"

****

In addition to the items listed above, each agency will have its own special set of needs that could be met by individuals who do not want to be on the board. And, of course, there are many creative, talented people who will think of things to do that would never have occurred to you—or us. Use your own imagination and be open to their suggestions.

The point is there are many ways of contributing to a nonprofit. Don't shut someone out just because they don't want to be on the board. And, as we said before, some of the best board members we know got started with the agency in a different capacity. Eventually, they had such a vested interest in the organization and its mission that they took the next logical step—they joined its governing body.

LETTERS AND BROCHURES TO HELP YOU RECRUIT GREAT BOARD MEMBERS:

The important written materials
you will need

9

Throughout this guide, we have discussed the need for mission statements, brochures, letters and news releases designed to help recruit board members. This section contains samples of all of these items. We will use a fictitious agency name, Adolfo Street Agency, as our nonprofit.

You are more than welcome to use these samples to suit your needs. If you would like us to take a look at your drafts, we will be happy to do so free of charge (please see Resources Section for details).

I. MISSION STATEMENT, BRIEF AGENCY HISTORY AND PROGRAM OVERVIEW
This is a multipurpose and fundamental document. It will help you with board recruitment, as an introduction to potential funding sources, the media and the community at large. The overview has only one page of text. You can print it all on one page as a flyer or fold it into a pamphlet. In either case, use pictures or catchy graphics (here is a good place to show off that striking and distinctive agency logo).

ADOLFO STREET AGENCY
1234 MAIN STREET
CENTERTOWN, USA
(555) 555-1234

ADOLFO STREET AGENCY (ASA), a nonprofit agency, was
started in 1983 by a group of citizens in Centertown and the
surrounding communities who felt that low-income seniors and
pre-school children in the area were not receiving adequate
nutrition. The agency opened its doors in late 1983 with a
breakfast and lunch program Monday through Friday. In 1985, the
agency expanded its services to include Saturday, Sunday and
evening meals.

ASA's mission statement is:
*"To promote good health for the low-income seniors and pre-school children
from low-income families in Jasper County by providing them with free,
nutritious and balanced meals 365 days a year."*

ASA has an annual budget of $422,000. It receives federal and
state funds and private donations. Many restaurants and supermar-
kets in Jasper County donate food to the organization.

Last year, ASA served 52,000 meals to seniors and 48,000 meals to
pre-school children.

ADOLFO STREET AGENCY needs your help to continue its
important work. Please consider donating your time as a board
member or a volunteer, making a financial contribution or just
learning more about us. Call us or stop by the agency. We would
be glad to show you around.

****

Let's look at this sheet for a moment. It gives a very
brief history so that anyone reading it will know why
the agency was started. It gives a short, distilled
version of its mission so the reader will know what
the agency wants to accomplish. It discloses, with-

out going into painful detail, the agency's budget. It lists the accomplishments of the previous year. It draws the reader in with a plea for help. It finishes with a friendly invitation.

Because this is simply a brief agency overview, it is a good idea to have a more detailed explanation of each of the major points on back up pages. For the fiscally minded, a corresponding sheet showing a pie chart with the percentages of federal, state and private funds and the amount spent in administration and direct services would be a very good idea.

Another page showing the number of meals served to each group by month would be highly effective (especially if shown on a bar graph). At the bottom would be a brief statement discussing the different nutritional needs of each of these groups and how these needs are addressed through the meals provided.

A third sheet would expand upon the agency's mission statement with more detailed goals, objectives and activities. A fourth could detail some of the nutrition-related health problems facing low-income seniors and pre-school children in the area before the agency opened.

These back up sheets would not be handed out to prospective board candidates or volunteers unless they asked for them. Many won't. However, if they do, nothing makes a better impression than being able to whip out more detailed information. Even on these back up sheets, however, never become too wordy or elaborate. Save the excruciating (albeit important) and painstaking, fine-print detail for another day and audience.

Consider your reader. Pack as much as you can into as few words as possible. Stick to the important stuff. End with a friendly, non-intimidating invitation. Make the typeface clear, bold and easy to read. Choose a good, strong but not overpowering paper color. No neon pinks, please! Always include your address and telephone number so they know where to reach you. If there is one person who is easily available to answer phone calls or to escort visitors around, list that person's name.

Notice we used the agency's initials after we spelled out the name at the beginning. If your organization's initials make a catchy acronym, go for it. However, if the full name of our fictitious agency were Adolfo Street Society, we would have avoided using just the initials for obvious reasons.

II. BOARD RECRUITMENT FLYER OR PAM-PHLET

This flyer or pamphlet (depending on how you have it printed) should be your key selling piece. It may be sent to prospects with a personalized letter or it may be handed out alone. This is the flyer you would leave with the realtor, church groups and others who may spot good candidates. Finally, you should always carry several copies with you in case you meet someone who would be just perfect to sit on your board.

****

ADOLFO STREET AGENCY
1234 MAIN STREET
CENTERTOWN, USA
(555) 555-1234

PLEASE CONSIDER JOINING THE BOARD OF
DIRECTORS OF ADOLFO STREET AGENCY.

ADOLFO STREET AGENCY (ASA) is a nonprofit organization governed by a volunteer board of directors. We currently have vacancies on the board that we need to fill with qualified, dedicated and interested people.

This pamphlet lists the most common questions we receive about the board and what it is like to be a board member. Please read it over. If you are still interested, please call us or stop by the agency. We will be happy to answer any other questions you may have.

1. WHAT IS THE GOAL OF ASA?

ASA is a nonprofit agency started in 1983. Its mission is to promote good health for low-income seniors and pre-school children from low-income families in Jasper County by providing them with free, nutritious and balanced meals 365 days a year.

2. WHAT DO THE BOARD MEMBERS DO?

The board of directors is the governing body of ASA. The board sets the overall policy and goals which are then carried out by the staff.

The ASA board meets on the second Thursday of every month at 7:00 pm. Meetings usually last about two hours. In addition, there are a few special events (such as our annual open house in December and the board retreat in July) which board members attend.

3. ARE BOARD MEMBERS PAID?

Board members are volunteers and do not get a salary. However, we do pay for all of your travel and meal costs to attend the meetings. We will also reimburse you for your child care costs if you need to hire a baby sitter.

Even though board members do not receive a salary, there are many benefits to sitting on our board. Just some of them are:

*It is an excellent way to help your community.
*You will develop or enhance your skills in budgeting, management, supervision and many other areas.
*You will have the opportunity to attend conferences in different and exciting cities around the country. Your expenses to attend these conferences are paid for by the agency.
*You will be working with some of the most interesting and important people in this community.

92

4. WOULD I HAVE TO MAKE SPEECHES?

Not unless you want to. Some of our board members do make presentations on behalf of the agency. However, most do not.

5. WHAT IF I HAVE TO MISS A MEETING EVERY ONCE IN A WHILE?

Most of our board members are unable to make every meeting. They are busy, active people! However, we ask our members to attend as many meetings as possible and to arrange their schedules so they can be there. As part of the governing body of the agency, you are very important to us.

6. I AM VERY INTERESTED IN WHAT ASA DOES, BUT I DON'T KNOW A LOT ABOUT IT. WILL I GET ANY INFORMATION ABOUT THE AGENCY AND ABOUT BEING A BOARD MEMBER?

Absolutely. We provide a basic orientation session for all new board members. In addition, there is an annual board training session conducted by an excellent consultant. We also give board members a manual with all of the important information they need to know about the agency. Finally, board members are always welcome to call or make an appointment with the Executive Director, Samuel Gallantin, to go over any aspect of the agency's operation.

7. ARE THE BOARD MEETINGS VERY FORMAL?

Not at all. They are important and the board members are there to conduct business. However, they are also interesting and fun. The board members are very professional but, at the same time, relaxed and casual.

The best way to see what we mean is to attend a board meeting yourself. You are more than welcome to come to our next meeting and observe the board in action. Remember: the meetings are held on the second Thursday of every month at 7:00 pm. Most of them are held at the ASA office in our conference room. However, it would be a good idea if you called us the day before to be sure the meeting has not been canceled and to confirm the location. We would love to have you visit us.

8. WHOM SHOULD I CALL IF I HAVE MORE QUESTIONS AND WANT TO LEARN MORE ABOUT WHAT THE AGENCY DOES?

Please call Samuel Gallantin, Executive Director at 555 - 1234 or Trish Garcia, President of the Board of Directors at 555-4321. They would be very happy to give you more information or to arrange a visit of the agency office or the meal sites.

WE HAVE A GREAT AGENCY, BUT WE NEED YOU TO HELP CONTINUE OUR IMPORTANT WORK FOR SOME OF THE MOST VULNERABLE CITIZENS IN OUR COMMUNITY. PLEASE CALL US TODAY!

****

Let's look closely at this one, too. Unlike the first sheet, this pamphlet focuses almost exclusively on the board of directors instead of the agency. There is a brief review of the mission at the beginning, but that is about it. The purpose is to ask people to sit on the board and our pamphlet wastes no time in getting down to work.

It would be perfectly appropriate to hand this one out with the first sheet which does talk about the agency in more detail. While a small portion of the information is repeated in both, they are quite different. Besides, repetition of key points is a good idea and a basic principle in advertising.

We used the question-and-answer format for several reasons. First, we have found it to be very effective not only in board recruitment pamphlets but in a number of other informational brochures as well. It focuses the reader on specific points. It breaks up the text so it does not become boring. You, the writer, can direct the way the reader thinks about the subject. You also set yourself up for success—a question has been asked and you answer it succinctly and completely, giving the reader the impression you know your stuff (which, of course, you do).

The question and answer format also allows you to articulate things the reader wants to know but doesn't want to ask. Are board members paid? Do I have to make speeches? What if I miss meetings? I don't know a lot about this agency or being on the board— is that ok? By saying, as we did in the beginning, that these are common questions, you make them feel more comfortable.

The question-and-answer style lets you sneak in important information that otherwise might be hard to incorporate gracefully. Right from the start, you are laying the groundwork for proper board conduct. Sure it's ok if you miss a meeting every once in a while, you are telling them, but you should plan on being there most of the time. Board members are always free to call the executive director (implying it is not appropriate for them to call the rest of the staff).

The tone of this pamphlet is direct but casual—very similar to the tone of the rest of this book and our other publications. The point, of course, is that the style in which your pamphlet is written should not be left to chance. It should reflect the tone and atmosphere of your agency. Perhaps your organization is more formal. If so, while you can still use the question-and-answer format very effectively, you would probably not start off your answers with sentences like "Absolutely" or "Not at all" as we did.

Our bias, of course, is toward a more informal style— we think it makes people much more comfortable. However, you should never be condescending, patronizing or unprofessional. In any case, the tone and style of your promotional materials should be consistent with the way in which your agency board and staff conduct themselves.

Did you notice how and when the pamphlet changed?. It started off talking about board members as "they" and "their" but shifted into "you" and "your" by the third sentence. That was deliberate. You bring them into the picture which is the first step to getting them to join. However, it finishes with another plea (remember, don't assume they have joined until they tell you they will) for them to consider being on the board.

A final note about the pamphlet: The current board (again, deliberate) was praised, directly or indirectly, in several places. An indirect compliment came right at the beginning. ". . .we need to fill with qualified, dedicated and interested people." There is a strong implication that the existing board members are also qualified, dedicated, etc. There is a direct compliment in the answers to the third and fourth questions . . . "You will be working with some of the most interesting and important people in this community" and "They [board members] are busy, active people!"

Of course, we assume you really mean these things, but it never hurts to make your current board members feel good about themselves and their role in the agency. This is another way to keep good board members once you have them.

If you can use a lot of this text as is, great. If not, list all of the things you want to tell them, put them in a logical order and turn each item into a question which you can answer. Then, answer the question and you have it made!

III. BOARD RECRUITMENT FLYER OR PAMPHLET FOR THE AGENCY'S CLIENTS

In our section on recruitment strategies, we

said it was important to develop a special pamphlet to recruit the agency's clients. They know a lot about the agency that no one, not even you, knows—what it is really like to get services from the agency! For that reason, they have a unique contribution to make to your board. You need to stress that point in your recruitment material.

Second, there are some issues unique to clients who serve as board members. These should also be addressed. However, the question-and-answer format can be used and many of the questions will be the same for any potential board member.

****

ADOLFO STREET AGENCY
1234 MAIN STREET
CENTERTOWN, USA
(555) 555-1234

YOU (OR SOMEONE IN YOUR FAMILY) ARE A CLIENT OF ADOLFO STREET AGENCY. THAT MAKES YOU VERY IMPORTANT TO US. SO IMPORTANT, IN FACT, THAT WE WOULD LIKE YOU TO THINK ABOUT BEING ON OUR BOARD OF DIRECTORS.

As a nonprofit organization, ADOLFO STREET AGENCY (ASA) is run by a volunteer board of directors. We currently have vacancies on the board that we would like to fill with qualified, dedicated and interested agency clients.
This pamphlet lists the most common questions and answers about the board and what it is like to be a board member. Please read it over. If you are still interested, please let the receptionist know you would like to talk to someone about being on the board. We will be happy to answer any other questions you may have.

1. WHAT IS THE GOAL OF ASA?
ASA was started in 1983 to provide nutritious and free meals to low-income seniors and pre-school children from low-

income families in all parts of Jasper County. With these meals, which are served 365 days a year, seniors and pre-school children have a greater chance of having good health and fewer illnesses resulting from poor nutrition.

2. WHAT DO THE BOARD MEMBERS DO?

The board of directors is the governing body of ASA. The board sets the overall policy and goals which are then carried out by the staff.

The ASA board meets on the second Thursday of every month at 7:00 pm. Meetings usually last about two hours. In addition, there are a few special events (such as our annual open house in December and the board retreat in July) which board members attend.

3. WHY DOES THE AGENCY WANT CLIENTS TO SIT ON THE BOARD?

For several reasons. First, the people who receive services from our agency know our strengths and weaknesses better than anyone else. Second, it is always important for clients to play a major role on the governing body of a community-based agency. This is your organization and you should have a strong voice in how it is run.

Third, our funding sources require that at least one-third of our board be our clients. However, even if that were not a requirement, this agency is committed to client leadership.

4. ARE BOARD MEMBERS PAID?

Board members are volunteers and do not get a salary. However, we do pay all of your travel and meal costs to attend the meetings. We will also reimburse you for your child care costs if you need to hire a baby sitter.

Even though board members do not receive a salary, there are many benefits to sitting on our board. Just some of them are:

*It is an excellent way to help your community.
*It is the best way for you to have a say in how the agency is run. Remember, ASA is there to serve you!
*You will develop or enhance your skills in a number of areas, such as budgeting, management, supervision and others.
*You will have the opportunity to attend conferences in

different and exciting cities around the country. Your expenses to
these conferences are paid for by the agency.

*You will be working with some of the most interesting
and important people in this community.

5. WOULD I HAVE TO MAKE SPEECHES?

Not unless you want to. A few board members do make
presentations on behalf of the agency. Some of our best and most
effective speakers have been clients who became board members.
However, this is not a requirement and you do not have to make
any speeches unless you want to.

6. WHAT IF I HAVE TO MISS A MEETING EVERY ONCE IN A WHILE?

Most of our board members are unable to make every
single meeting. They are busy, active people! However, we ask our
members to attend as many meetings as possible and to arrange
their schedules so they can be there. As part of the governing body
of the agency, you are very important to us.

7. WHAT IF I DISAGREE WITH SOME OF THE OTHER BOARD MEMBERS WHO ARE NOT CLIENTS. WILL THAT HAVE AN EFFECT ON THE WAY I AM TREATED BY THE AGENCY?

Not at all. Your role as board member will have no effect
whatsoever on the services you or your family receive at ASA.
There are always differences of opinion among board members.
That is healthy and we encourage everyone to express their views.

8. I KNOW A LOT ABOUT THE AGENCY BUT I DON'T HAVE ANY EXPERIENCE BEING A BOARD MEMBER. WILL I GET SOME INFORMATION OR TRAINING?

Yes! All new board members get an orientation session
on being a board member. We also work with an excellent
consultant who gives an annual training session to the entire board.
You will get a manual with a lot of helpful information. And board
members are always welcome to make an appointment with the
Executive Director, Samuel Gallantin, to go over anything they do
not understand or wish to discuss further.

9. ARE THE BOARD MEETINGS VERY FORMAL?

Not in this agency! They are important and the board
members are there to conduct business. However, they are also

interesting and fun. The board members are very professional but, at the same time, relaxed and casual.

The best way to see what we mean is to attend a board meeting yourself. (By the way, even if you are not interested in being a board member, you are always welcome to attend a board meeting. They are open to the public and we always encourage ASA's clients to see how the agency is run.) Remember, the meetings are held on the second Thursday of every month at 7:00 pm. Most of them are held at the ASA office in our conference room. Notices of the meetings are posted at all of the meal sites on the bulletin boards so you will always know when and where the next meeting will be held. However, it would be a good idea if you called us the day before to be sure the meeting has not been canceled.

10. WILL THERE BE ANY REPERCUSSIONS IF I DECIDE NOT TO JOIN THE BOARD?
No! We don't want you to feel pressured to join. Being a board member is not for everybody. It takes time and effort. You are under no obligation whatsoever and you will continue to be one of our valued clients.

11. WHOM SHOULD I CALL IF I HAVE MORE QUESTIONS?
Please call Samuel Gallantin, Executive Director at 555-1234 or Trish Garcia, President of the Board of Directors at 555-4321. (By the way, Trish is a client as well. She has been coming to our Northeast site for three years for breakfast. She would be happy to tell you what it is like to be a board member and a client of ASA.)

WE HAVE A GREAT AGENCY, BUT WE NEED YOU TO HELP CONTINUE OUR IMPORTANT WORK FOR YOU AND OUR OTHER CLIENTS. PLEASE CONSIDER JOINING OUR BOARD!

****

As you can see, there are some additional questions for clients. It is very important to reassure them there will be no repercussions if they don't join the board. If they do join, they must feel free to voice their opinions. We have found these points to be the major concerns of clients who are considering joining the board.

While some of the questions are exactly the same, the answers may be slightly different. You must always remember your audience and make your pitch accordingly.

It goes without saying that Trish Garcia gave her permission to mention she was a client of the agency before this was put in the pamphlet. Most client/board members are proud of their dual role and will have no objections to using this information to attract other clients. But check first.

IV.   BASIC BOARD RECRUITMENT (INVITATION) LETTER

Here is your first direct, personal pitch to a potential board member. Good or bad, it will make a lasting impression.

****

January 5, 19xx

Sandra McFarlane
4567 Aster Drive
Centertown, USA

Dear Ms. McFarlane:

Your name was given to me by James Andover who said you may be interested in joining the board of directors of Adolfo Street Agency. James said you are a dedicated and talented person with a strong interest in helping seniors and children. Because our agency serves both of these groups, our board and staff would be very pleased to have you serve on the board of directors.

Attached is a brief overview of the agency and a pamphlet written especially for prospective board members. The board meets on the first Thursday of every month at 7:00 pm. Meetings generally last for two hours.

I will call you next week to see if you would be interested in becoming a board member. I am sure you would find the experience extremely rewarding.

In the meantime, if you have any questions, please feel free to call me. Thank you for your time.

Sincerely,

Trish Garcia

Trish Garcia
President, Board of Directors
Adolfo Street Agency

****

This is a straightforward letter. Because you have the pamphlets to go along with it, you don't have to cram everything in the letter. Instead, you can focus on the person you are trying to recruit. (However, we do recommend you tell them how frequently the board meets. People seem unable to concentrate on anything else until they know what kind of time commitment you are asking for.)

While the message is clear—we want you on our board and you will be glad you joined—it is not particularly pushy. The letter could be modified to target specific people. For example, if the agency provided day-care and the letter were addressed to that professor in early-childhood development we talked about earlier, the first paragraph would go something like . . .

You have an excellent reputation for your work in early-childhood development. Dr. Brent recently told me that you are very interested in the role day-care centers play in the social develop-

ment of pre-school children from disadvantaged families. Because
we provide day-care to low-income families, we need someone with
your expertise on our governing body. Therefore, we would be
extremely pleased if you would consider joining our board of
directors.

If the letter were directed to a client of the agency, you would reinforce the importance of their role on the governing body. If Trish Garcia were writing the letter, it would be very effective to reinforce the fact that she too is an agency client.

Always use another person's name if you can to provide an introduction. It is much more personal and will make them want to read on. Plus, it gives you something in common. You both know James Andover. You both know Dr. Brent.

We find the simple, direct approach in letters to be the most effective of all. The pamphlets and brochures you enclose with the letter take care of the rest.

Finally, if your letter says you are going to call next week to follow up on the letter, be sure to do so. It is the first opportunity you have to show them you can be trusted to come through on the commitments (no matter how small) you have made. We have known more than one board prospect who said they were waiting for the follow up call that never came. They decided the agency wasn't that interested in them after all.

V. NEWS RELEASE

As we said before, a news release is an indirect way of recruiting board members. In fact, a good one should help you in a number of areas. The trick is to use them wisely. No decent newspaper is going to use your news releases if you send one in every time a board member sneezes or a staff person burps.

However, if you find out you got that multi-million dollar grant you applied for last Fall, grab your pen (or word processor) and get to work! Never let a solid-gold opportunity pass by without doing a release.

****

FOR IMMEDIATE RELEASE: (DATE)
CONTACT: SAMUEL GALLANTIN,
EXECUTIVE DIRECTOR
ADOLFO STREET AGENCY
(505) 555-1234

LOCAL AGENCY RECEIVES USDA GRANT

Adolfo Street Agency received word on Tuesday that it will be awarded four hundred thousand dollars ($400,000) from the US Department of Agriculture for a demonstration program to provide meals to low-income seniors. "The difference between this demonstration project and our current meal program is we will be able to show that if you personalize the meals to each person, you will prevent more serious medical problems down the road," said Executive Director Samuel Gallantin. Added Board President Trish Garcia, who has been receiving meals at Adolfo Street Agency for the past three years, "We try to meet everyone's needs. But with our current budget, it is impossible to do so. Now we can hire a nutritionist to focus on the needs of each of our clients."

Research shows that senior citizens have far fewer health problems if their diets are tailored to their individual conditions. "For example," said Ms. Garcia, "Now if someone has hypertension, we can help deal with that through the meals we serve. It just makes common sense."

Samuel Gallantin praised the staff and board of Adolfo Street Agency for the hard work in preparing the application. "It was a very competitive process," he said. "We were going up against some high-powered agencies in the big cities. But everyone pulled together to show we could do some terrific things with this money."

The agency currently provides meals seven days a week at six sites in Jasper County. Low-income senior citizens and pre-school children from low-income families are eligible for free meals.

****

News releases usually start off with the statement "For immediate release." The effectiveness is gone if it sits around for a long time. The phrase "as stale as yesterday's news" says it all. They should be double-spaced.

The first paragraph starts out with all of the five basics—*who* (Adolfo Street Agency), *what* (an award of four hundred thousand dollars) *where* (Adolfo Street Agency again—the repetition is not a problem, in fact it is a plus), *when* (Tuesday) and *why* (to provide personalized meals for senior citizens). The rest of the release simply reinforces what was said in the first paragraph.

When the release is hand-delivered or faxed,the folks at the newspaper don't have to wade through a lot of material to find out what happened. They can tell immediately whether it is newsworthy. If your news release is well written, you will often find it used word for word in the newspaper. After a while, every single one of our releases was used without any changes whatsoever.

The publicity doesn't have to stop there. The initial write up in the paper may lead to other, more in-depth articles about the agency. Local radio and television stations (their staff scour the newspaper daily for interesting items) may call you and ask for an interview or (in the case of television stations) to bring a camera crew over to see the agency in action. After a news release makes the papers, be prepared to handle calls. Alert the staff and board so they know what to do if someone calls for more information or an interview.

Again, board recruitment is not the primary focus. A paper would have to be pretty desperate to run an article with a headline like **"ADOLFO STREET AGENCY LOOKING FOR GREAT BOARD MEM-BERS."** However, the publicity you get from a release like the one we wrote above will do wonders for your recruitment efforts. You could attach copies of the article to your board recruitment letter for added effect. We have all heard the old adage "Don't believe everything you read." However, it is a fact of life that most people attach a high degree of credibility to the written word.

Be prepared to turn anything and everything positive and newsworthy about your agency into a news release. Be prepared for the follow up. Use that momentum to recruit board members before the fanfare has died down. Keep a complete file of all newspaper clippings to use for future recruitment drives.

VI. ALTERNATE NEWS RELEASE

There is another type of release you can use under special circumstances that could help with board recruitment. This one is trickier to pull off well and it takes practice. You may decide you want to call attention to the issue your agency is addressing (in our example, the problems facing low-income seniors and pre-school children from low-income families in getting adequate nutrition) to raise funds, community support or just general awareness. If you do, keep board recruitment in mind as you write the release.

****

FOR IMMEDIATE RELEASE: (DATE)
CONTACT: SAMUEL GALLANTIN,
EXECUTIVE DIRECTOR
ADOLFO STREET AGENCY
(555) 555-1234

POOR NUTRITION AMONG THE POOR LEADS TO
MAJOR HEALTH PROBLEMS

You are what you eat. There is a lot of truth in that old saying. But you

don't need to convince the board and staff of ADOLFO STREET

AGENCY. This nonprofit, which has been serving low-income

seniors and pre-school children from low-income families in Jasper

County for over ten years, knows exactly what happens when their clients don't get good nutrition. "We have new clients all of the time who have been hospitalized for all sorts of illnesses related to poor nutrition, " said ADOLFO STREET Board President Trish Garcia. "Their doctors tell us these elderly people would have a lot fewer problems if they could eat three good meals a day, seven days a week." For pre-school children, the problems are just as bad. "Inadequate nutrition can have permanent damaging effects. These children have at least one strike against them before they ever get to first grade." That is what ADOLFO STREET AGENCY is all about. Nutritious, balanced and free meals are served to low-income seniors and pre-school children from low-income families at six different sites around Jasper County 7 days a week, 365 days a year. The agency has a volunteer board of directors and a small, paid staff working very hard to make sure their clients don't go without meals—ever. "If the temperature is minus 15 degrees, we will be here. If they can't get to us, we will find a way to get to them," said Executive Director Samuel Gallantin. "Our board, staff and volunteers are extremely commit-ted."

It appears to be paying off. Mr. and Mrs. Nantes, both in their 80's, have been coming to the State Avenue site for almost five years. "Before we came here, both of us had terrible colds and bronchitis every winter," said Mr. Nantes. "Our resistance was down and we both ended up in the hospital at least three times. And while we still get colds, they are a lot better. Our doctor is very pleased."

Board President Trish Garcia, who also gets at least ten meals a week from the agency, agrees. "Good nutrition is essential for good health," she said. "And while it won't cure every illness in the world, you haven't got a prayer if you can't eat right."

****

Why are these types of releases harder to write? Because in public relations you need to balance the gloom-and-doom message (Any problem worth tackling is, almost by definition, depressing and people don't like to be depressed.) with an element of hope. If you can't leave them with something positive, don't try this kind of news release.

Although you would start off with "For immediate release," this one is not time-sensitive. The paper may not pick up on it right away. However, if they don't have a lot of other hot items to cover, they may run the piece. Or, they may turn it over to the features editor to do a more in-depth article.

Although quite a different animal, our second release does not abandon the principles we discussed earlier. The entire issue is laid out in the first paragraph. The last paragraph could be cut without killing the piece. We still have our who (low-income elderly and pre-school children), what (need adequate nutrition), and why (to stay healthy). The when and where are less important here because of the nature of the piece; it is not reporting a specific, single event.

By the way—if you use statistics or give examples of a problem, make them as local as possible. If we had a dollar for every report that quoted national figures but omitted local statistics, we would be rich. National figures are important to put a community's dilemma in perspective, but they should never be the focus of your piece.

How does this piece help with board recruitment? It shows the board as dedicated and committed. Other dedicated and committed people in the community (with or without a cause) will definitely take notice. And while you are not making a direct pitch to get them to join, there is an underlying (marketing and advertising experts call it subliminal) message that says "The people who belong to our board of directors are good, caring people. That makes them special. If you are concerned about others, you belong on our board."

One more time: The primary purpose of both of these releases is not to recruit board members. But they provide a wonderful opportunity to reinforce, underscore and bolster your other, more direct recruitment efforts.

VII. PUBLIC SERVICE ANNOUNCEMENT (PSA) 30 SECONDS

A public service announcement (commonly referred to as a PSA) is a short piece which is read aloud on radio and television. Radio and television stations must do a certain number of these each month. It is part of their responsibility to the communities they serve. They are free to qualified agencies.

Writing a PSA is totally different than writing a news release or other piece that is meant to be read in a newspaper. A PSA should sound good. And while that may seem like an obvious statement, we cringe at some of the announcements we hear. There are some basic principles to remember. First, they must be short (we will give an example of a 30 and a 60-second PSA below). And, because they are short, they must be concise, to the point and easy to read aloud. Even trained announcers cannot handle a PSA that does not allow them to take a breath for an entire 30 or 60 seconds!

If your PSA is not good, the announcer (or someone) will edit it. No one wants to sound like an idiot over the air. However, they can botch the editing job and the result may not convey what you want. Make sure it is good before you ever send it in.

****

Are you looking for a way to help your community? A chance to meet some of the most interesting and dynamic people in Jasper County? ADOLFO STREET AGENCY has openings on its board of directors. ADOLFO STREET provides meals to low-income seniors and pre-school children 365 days a year. Call us—you will never regret it. Call 555-1234 for more information on how to join. That's 555-1234.

****

Thirty seconds is not a lot of time. You need to get the most out of it. You start off by grabbing their attention with the benefits of joining (even, if you will notice, before they know you are asking them to join something). Then you tell them how they can get these benefits (the agency has openings on its board of directors). Once you have their attention, you tell them a little about the agency itself. You finish by telling them what to do. And then you tell them again.

Notice we repeated the telephone number twice. People may not catch it the first time. A good announcer, unless he or she is running out of time, will repeat it slowly the second time.(Unlike the other materials, you would not put the area code in a PSA. First, it takes too much time. Second, it is unnecessary. Your board members are going to be local. Only if you live in a city in which there are a dozen area codes right next to each other would you need to include the area code. In those cases, you would also want to remind them of the general location of your agency.)

Our sentences are short enough to allow the announcer to take a breath somewhere in the middle. The phrasing sounds good when read aloud. We know—we read it aloud several times and fined tuned it. We also got a timer to be sure it did not exceed 30 seconds. In fact, a PSA should be slightly less than 30 (or 60) seconds. You need to allow for the difference in readers—television and radio time is very carefully calibrated. If they need to cut away to something else, they will—even if it means your phone number is chopped off.

If you have any names that may be mispronounced, list those at the top and spell them out phonetically. A good announcer will check the release to see if there are any words he or she does not know how to pronounce. But don't leave that to chance. If your agency name is very long, you can use an acronym or abbreviation (notice we said Adolfo Street instead of Adolfo Street Agency the second time) provided the announcer first says the entire agency name.

VIII. PUBLIC SERVICE ANNOUNCEMENT (PSA) 60 SECONDS

The 60-second PSA allows you more time for crucial details. However, the principles are the same. It should sound crisp when read aloud...

****

Are you looking for a way to help your community? A chance to meet some of the most interesting and dynamic people in Jasper County? ADOLFO STREET AGENCY has openings on its board of directors for dedicated, caring board members. No prior experience is necessary and we will give you all of the training you need. ADOLFO STREET is a nonprofit organization providing meals to low-income seniors and pre-school children from low-income families. We serve meals 365 days a year throughout Jasper County. Call us—you will never regret it. Being a board member will not take up a lot of your time but the rewards are tremendous. Call 555-1234 for more information or to arrange for a visit. That's 555-1234. Find out how you can make a difference!

****

In this version, we added material to make it more attractive to potential board members . . . "No prior experience is necessary and we will give you all of the training you need." We also talked a little more about the agency. Finally, we reinforced (with more detail) why they should call.

The shorter Public Service Announcements force you to distill all of your key points into the fewest words possible. If you have more time (60 instead of 30 seconds), don't let your piece lose its focus or its punch.

Find out from the stations how long their PSA spots are. They may be different (for example, 20 or 45 seconds). Stay well within those limits.

Be sure to ask the station manager (or designated contact person) how much lead time they need. If they want four weeks, give them four weeks. There are many causes competing for this valuable air time and you must abide by their time frames.

Many stations have community affairs programs in which they highlight an issue of local concern and interest. These can be 15 or 30 minute segments and they are fantastic opportunities to get a lot of exposure for your agency. If you have presented your organization professionally through PSA's and, equally as important, through your contact with the station personnel, you stand a good chance of getting on one of these segments.

The moral of the story is that every opportunity to present and represent your agency well can help you gain other invaluable publicity. And, this, of course, will help your board recruitment efforts.

IX. OTHER WAYS TO HELP

Our final piece is the "Plan B" pamphlet in which we discuss other things people can do to help the agency if they do not want to join the board. You should be able to give it to board prospects who say no as well as to people you did not even attempt to recruit for board positions.

However, you would probably hand it out after (or at the same time) you give the person the very first (mission statement, agency history and program overview) pamphlet. It saves you from repeating the agency information all over again.

****

ADOLFO STREET AGENCY
1234 MAIN STREET
CENTERTOWN, USA
(555) 555-1234

Thank you for your interest in our agency. In this pamphlet, we list just a few of the many ways you can help us carry out our important work. We know you are very busy but we hope you will consider one of these activities or projects. Your time and talent will go a long way to help the low-income seniors and pre-school children in Jasper County.

1. YOU CAN BE A VOLUNTEER

We need volunteers at each of our six sites to help prepare and serve the meals to our seniors and pre-school children. You can choose one, two, three, four or more days a month (depending upon how much time you can give). Before you start, you will go through a three-hour training session with other new volunteers.

This is a wonderful way to work with seniors and young children. Many of our volunteers have been with us for several years and they tell us they would not trade the experience for anything in the world.

If you want to volunteer time but want a quieter setting, you could work in our administrative office on Main Street. We always need help preparing large mail-outs, answering phones or making copies.

2. HELP US RAISE FUNDS

Do you have a knack for raising funds? We need you! We try to have several fund-raising events and campaigns every year. We hold benefit dinners, bake sales and raffles. We target several foundations each year and we solicit individual donations from businesses and private citizens.

If you have raised funds in the past or if you have a great idea on how we can might generate some money for the organization, we would love to talk to you.

3. BECOME A FRIEND OF ADOLFO STREET AGENCY

Even though our agency does very important work, we can use all of the friends we can get! We need you to speak out for us when we go before the City Council and the County Commission. We need your support at hearings and at neighborhood meetings. If your other obligations do not permit you to become a volunteer, please consider becoming a friend of our agency. It won't take much time and you will help us more than you know.

4. HAVE YOU EVER WANTED TO TRY YOUR HAND AS A LOBBYIST?

Agencies like ours don't hire professional lobbyists the way the big businesses and special interests do. But we need people to lobby for more funds for programs like ours throughout the state and the country.

Each year, the U.S. Congress and our State Legislature (on the legislative side) and the President and our Governor (on the executive side) must consider how much money they will budget for programs like ours. They need to hear from a lot of people about how important these services are. And while they listen to our clients and they listen to us, nothing makes a stronger impression than knowing that the community in general (remember, you are taxpayers!) thinks this is a very worthwhile cause.

You could write letters to your elected officials. And, if you really want to get involved, you could meet with your state senators and representatives. If you are really brave and adventurous, you could go to Washington!

5. AND LOTS OF OTHER PROJECTS . . .

If you can paint, cook, design, build or fix things, straighten out messes, organize—we need you! Periodically, we have special, one-time-only projects that require people of many different talents. Let us know what you can do and we will keep you in mind the next time one of these comes up.

6. NO TIME? WHAT ABOUT SOME MONEY?

If you haven't got an extra minute in your day to spare, don't worry. We understand. But if you still want to help, we can always use donations. Our budget is only partially funded with public dollars. The rest comes from contributions. Or, if you have something of value we can raffle, that would be just as good.

We have only touched on the ways you can help ASA. You can probably think of a hundred more. Please call us today if you are interested in working with us. Or, just call to have your name put on our list to receive our free monthly newsletter. We always talk about what is going on in the agency and how you can help

Thank you!

****

As you can see, we simply took the list from the earlier section and turned it into "user-friendly" language. Keep it short, simple and direct. Get them on your mailing list and be sure to mention different ways they can help in every newsletter. However, don't belabor the point or people will tune you out. If someone calls or stops by with an offer to help, be prepared to answer their questions. Just as we suggested with the very first pamphlet, you might want to have a more in-depth fact sheet to go with each of the major topics we listed above.

THE END

It is time to stop. We sincerely hope this guide has given you some ideas and strategies you can use in your own board recruitment efforts. Please consult the appendices for additional resources and services.

We want to leave you with perhaps the most important point of this guide. Board recruitment and your efforts to keep good board members cannot, in fact must not be isolated activities in the operation of a nonprofit. Look at everything you do in relation to the agency as an important part of your board recruitment strategy. See if the way in which you are doing it will help or hurt your ability to get the people you want to serve on your governing body.

Good luck and let us know how it goes!

SELECT BIBLIOGRAPHY

BODY AND SOUL by Anita Roddick
Crown Publishers: 1991 A great book detailing the phenomenal growth of a for profit company with intelligence, ethics, heart and, of course, soul. What makes it particularly relevant for nonprofits is the thoughtful way Anita looked at the mission of the company at each step. By the way, she mentions several times that she is looking to collaborate with worthy nonprofits—something to check out!

CHASE'S ANNUAL EVENTS: SPECIAL DAYS, WEEKS AND MONTHS
Contemporary Books: 1990 This guide is just what it says. It lists special and commemorative events in just about every conceivable area. Use it to snag some great publicity.

CORPORATE LIFECYCLES by Ichak Adizes
Prentice Hall: 1988 A very detailed analysis of the lifecycles of businesses in the for profit world; however, nonprofits follow many of the same patterns. This is serious stuff, but we were struck by the amazing similarities between the businesses Dr. Adizes described and nonprofits we have known. It also gave us food for thought on the future of the agencies we are still involved with. An important book.

GROWING A BUSINESS by Paul Hawkins
Fireside: 1988 A book everyone in business, for profit or nonprofit, should read. It contains many useful (and we daresay brilliant) insights and, like Anita Roddick's book, reminds us that business can be ethical and compassionate. It is a joy to read.

HOW TO BECOME A GREAT BOARD MEMBER
by Dorian Dodson
Adolfo Street Publications: 1993 The companion guide to HOW TO RECRUIT GREAT BOARD MEMBERS, this book helps people decide whether or not to become board members and gives them all of the basic information they need to get started. Designed to take the mystery out of the process, the guide is short, friendly and to the point.

HOW TO PUT ON A GREAT CONFERENCE by Dorian Dodson
Adolfo Street Publications: 1992 An easy-to-use, comprehensive guide to putting on conferences, workshops or other events, this book is perfect for nonprofits. One national reviewer called it "the best small-scale book on conferences yet."

MARKETING WITHOUT ADVERTISING by Michael Phillips and Salli Rasberry
Nolo Press: 1990 This book provides hundreds of excellent ideas for anyone interested in promoting their business (including nonprofits) the right way. Read it even if you do advertise. By the way, Nolo Press has many great titles designed to help us non-lawyers navigate through the world of legalities.

ROBERT'S RULES OF ORDER 9th Edition by Henry Martin Robert III
Harper Collins: 1991 The most famous manual of parliamentary procedure of them all. This is a must-have book for any board member—especially the chairperson!

RESOURCES

The local United Way: Most large and mid-size communities are served by a United Way affiliate. They provide (or have access to) excellent board training and other useful sessions. We find their staff to be friendly and helpful—it is, of course, in their best interest to have strong nonprofits because United Way funds are awarded to nonprofits. See if you can make an appointment with one of the key staff and discuss your needs. They also have some of the best directories of services (including nonprofits) around.

Other strong nonprofits: Do you have a Big Brothers/Big Sisters affiliate in your community? An Association for Retarded Citizens? Habitat for Humanity or a Community Action Agency? These and other organizations are old pro's at the business of running nonprofits and they have access to national resources and information. Attend their board meetings, identify some of the movers and shakers and get to know them. They can (and usually will) help you develop your own board recruitment strategies.

Adolfo Street Publications: We will be very happy to review your pamphlets, flyers or letters. Unless you send us a huge book, this service is free of charge. Send the information you would like us to review (as well as any background material on your agency you have already developed) and a self-addressed, stamped envelope to:

Board Editor
Adolfo Street Publications
P.O. Box 490
Santa Fe, NM 87504-0490

We will also provide answers to your specific questions on board recruitment or related topics. Please put them in writing, however, so we can leave our phone lines free.

INDEX

About the Publisher

ADOLFO STREET PUBLICATIONS is a small, independent publishing company based in Santa Fe, New Mexico. We specialize in straightforward, easy to use books on community relations and interaction among people—especially those people who are trying to make this a better world.

We think books on community and human relations should be friendly, funny and should have a lot of common sense. We would love to know if you think we met our goal.

Please write or call:

Gene A. Valdes, Vice President
Adolfo Street Publications
Post Office Box 490
Santa Fe, New Mexico 87504-0490

Phone: (505) 986-2010
Fax: (505) 986-1353

About the Illustrator

Janice St. Marie has been an illustrator and designer since 1981. Her work has gained increased recognition and popularity throughout the Southwest, nationally and abroad. She lives in Santa Fe, New Mexico on ten pinon-covered acres with her husband, six cats, two dogs and assorted fish.